Recollections of an Excursion to the Monasteries of Alcobaça and Batalha

by William Beckford

With his original journal of 1794
and Introduction and Notes
by Boyd Alexander

'Memories of Portugal will always be the
memories nearest to my heart.' *Beckford in 1812*

CENTAUR PRESS
AN IMPRINT OF OPEN GATE PRESS
LONDON

This edition first published in 2006 by Centaur Press,
an imprint of Open Gate Press
51 Achilles Road, London NW6 1DZ

First edition published in 1835.
First Centaur Press edition published in 1972.

British Library Cataloguing-in-Publication Programme
A catalogue reference for this book is available from the
British Library.

ISBN: 0 900001 52 6

Printed and bound in Great Britain
by BookForce, Grantham, Lincs.

Advertisement

The other day, in examining some papers, I met with very slight notes of this Excursion. Flattering myself that, perhaps, they might not be totally unworthy of expansion, I invoked the powers of memory – and behold, up rose the whole series of recollections I am now submitting to that indulgent public, which has shown more favour to my former sketches than they merited.

LONDON,
June 1835.

Contents

Introduction

Odd, that until now there has been in England no printing of Beckford's *Excursion* as a separate volume since the first edition in 1835, although there have been three subsequent printings of it bound up with his *Sketches of Italy, Spain and Portugal* (short-titled hereafter as *Spain and Portugal*). Odd, because from time to time critics have reminded us of its importance in travel literature and of its unique qualities in this class of writing, for which it has always appealed to certain readers.

Whibley says it 'is the masterpiece of his experience and is so far embellished by memory and invention as to seem a work of pure imagination.'[1] Rose Macaulay, who is severe on Beckford's character and sharp in her judgements, admirably sums up its essential quality: 'For fact-seekers it is tantalizing; for those who are content to accept his narration as a lovely and amusing chain of incidents, humours and descriptions, partly memories, partly dreams, waking thoughts and inventions, the *Excursion* is almost without a rival . . . its conversations are ridiculous and gay; it is by someone who saw sharply, beautifully, with the artist's eye . . . to read it is to stroll, with a perceptive guide, through beautiful scenes and odd, amusing society. It never flags. ..'[2] Incidentally, Beckford, an artist *manqué*, often claims he saw things 'with the eye of an artist', although Lockhart reminds us that he also wrote his travel prose like 'a poet, and a great one too.'[3]

Miss Macaulay is quick to point out how different is his approach and quality from 'the prim, stilted, ponderous didactic style of most of his fellow-travellers.' So it is pointless laboriously to compare his impressions with theirs, although I shall show later how on one or two general points he is backed by his exactly contemporary traveller, 'that dull draughtsman Murphy'.

Some modern critics have analysed Beckford's method and its results when describing his best-known work *Vathek*, written in a short space of time in 1782, when he was twenty-one. They might almost equally well be describing the *Excursion*, written fairly quickly early in 1835 (perhaps beginning late in 1834), when he was seventy-four. Professor Elton, in his *Survey of English Literature,* writes of *Vathek*: '. . . the Eastern senses, wrought on by the drug imagination, expand and dream and build colossal toppling towers of pleasure and luxury; and then, finding how narrow after all is that infinite sphere, they fall back defeated, and rest on the pageantry of daily life, on the din of the bazaars and the quarrels of merchants, and on ingenious anecdote and proverb. Something of all this is felt in Beckford's inventions, and in no other writing of the time.'[4] This is an interesting but perhaps plausible and too charitable explanation of the contrast between the majestic settings and the tittle-tattle into which Beckford so often descends in his books.

Lockhart, in reviewing *Spain and Portugal* in 1834 (in terms which equally could apply to the *Excursion)*, gives a simpler explanation rooted in the contrasts in Beckford's character, so well brought out in his letters from Fonthill to his Portuguese secretary Franchi, who accompanied him to the monasteries.

After commenting on the poetic quality of the book, so 'unlike any book of travels *in prose* that exists in any European language', and on its profound melancholy blended with picturesque description, Lockhart points out that Beckford 'betrays in a thousand places a settled voluptuousness of temperament, and a capricious recklessness of self-indulgence, which will lead the world to identify him henceforth with his Vathek, . . . and then, that there may be no limit to the inconsistencies of such a strange genius, this spirit, at once so capable of the noblest enthusiasm and so dashed with the gloom of over-pampered luxury, can stoop to chairs and china, ever and anon, with the zeal of an auctioneer – revel in the design of a clock or a candlestick, and be as ecstatic about a fiddler or a soprano as the fools in Hogarth's *concert*. On such occasions he reminds us and will, we think, remind every one, of the Lord of Strawberry Hill. But even here all we have is on a grander scale. The oriental prodigality of his magnificence shines out even above the trifles. He buys a library where the other would have cheapened a missal. He is at least a male Horace Walpole; as superior to the 'silken Baron', as Fonthill, with its York-like tower embosomed among hoary forests, was to that silly band-box which still may be admired on the road to Twickenham.' Beckford would have been enraged at the comparison with 'the Pest of Strawberry Hill' (as he dubbed his rival collector), but delighted by the animadversion on Strawberry Hill itself, which he called 'a Gothick mouse-trap'.

Returning to a modern critic's analysis of *Vathek*, which so aptly fits the *Excursion*, Professor Daiches remarks: 'Its oriental setting enables Beckford to indulge an imagination sometimes fantastic, some times magnificent, sometimes humorous; he can raise exaggeration to the level of epic extravaganza. . . . only Beckford was able to use the remoteness of the setting as a justification of a new kind of probability in fiction: in *Vathek* he created and inhabited a world of ideal fantasy. The work had little real influence: it took a highly individual kind of imagination to use his materials as Beckford did.'[5] By the time that Beckford wrote in 1835, the life he described in the monasteries in 1794 was as remote as anything in *Vathek*: it had been sapped by the influence of the French Revolution; the philistine and atheistic armies of Napoleon had desecrated and badly damaged the buildings; and anti-clericalism had suppressed the monasteries in 1832.

Could Beckford really have sat down forty years later to describe his trip so minutely and vividly? Miss Macaulay definitely thinks not, and quotes his artful journalist's phrase when describing his interview with the Prince-Regent of Portugal (later King Joaõ VI): 'Let me observe, whilst the recollections of the interviews I have had with him remain fresh in my memory. . .' She is aware of his apparently mock-modest Preface which, like so much of his, has never been taken at its face-value: 'The other day, in examining some papers, I met with very slight notes of this Excursion. Flattering myself that, perhaps, they might not be totally unworthy of expansion, I invoked the powers of memory – and behold, up rose the whole series of recollections I am now submitting to that indulgent public, which has shown more favour to my former sketches than they merited'.

Her sharp comment on this seems fair: 'A characteristically Beckfordian falsification. The slight notes must have been a full narration, written at a time when its memory was still clear and sharp. No doubt it was added to, altered, faked up here and there; . . . but in essentials it must have been contemporary. The wealth of closely-observed (or beautifully invented) detail, the sharp loveliness of the descriptions, the life-like conversations, the richness of the fun, the irony and the poetry and the decoration, can neither be a memory forty years old suddenly invoked, nor the composition of a man in his mid-seventies; it has all the fresh power, poetry and enjoyment of youth.'

As she says, the book is remarkable as a tour de force of imagination with some basis in fact. But how much more remarkable if it was written off the cuff by a man of seventy-four who had not visited Portugal for thirty-five years (since 1799*)*.

So it is vital to establish when he wrote it. Like *Spain and Portugal* of 1834, was it a rehash and careful selection of a long daily journal? His fragmentary early drafts are in three separate lots in his Papers, grouped as found but put in modern folders. The first lot is jotted on the backs of letters received by him in 1834–5, and the handwriting of all three lots is of this unmistakable late period. Furthermore, the late Mr. James Babb, then Librarian of Yale, told me that he owned Beckford's copy of Prince Puckler-Muskau's *Tutti Frutti*, 1834, and that its fly-leaves, fore and aft, are covered by Beckford's tiny pencil notes which are an early or first draft of the *Excursion*. This is how many authors start to write a book germinating in their minds: they sieze any bit of paper to hand as ideas; phrases and situations occur to them; this is how Beckford began and sometimes kept up his 1787 *Journal in Portugal and Spain*, his 1823 mock *Epitaphs* and his *Liber Veritatis*, begun in 1828–9.

But we could still ask: was there a Journal on which these drafts are based and which they closely follow, merely working it up and perfecting it? There is indeed a genuine 1794 Journal, printed as an Appendix to this edition. I have described and commented on it fully elsewhere, so will only repeat one or two necessary points.[6] There is no reason to suppose that any part of this Journal has been destroyed or lost. It shows that he was too busy enjoying the monasteries to write anything during his stay there except on his last night at Alcobaça, when he made two notes on the small blank space on the torn half of the outside of a letter recently received from England (Monday 9th June, Seventh Day). As can be seen, these are very Beckfordian, being architectural details and the following typical observation: 'This evening a sleek friar with wanton eyes accompanied Franchi on the Jew's harp; I hear him twanging away at this moment.' This links up in an interesting but inconclusive way with the *Excursion*'s account of the clownish play on Inez de Castro which Beckford claims to have seen that evening at Alcobaça.

On and off during the earlier part of his life, whether in Savoy and Switzerland between 1777 and 1783, in England in 1779, or in Portugal in 1794, he began diaries or entries which quickly peter out, often (as in 1794) in mid-sentence. It was lucky for us and him that occasionally he was more persistent and disciplined – at the Grande Chartreuse in 1778, in Italy in 1780, in Portugal (and to begin with in Spain) in 1787–8, and at Aranjuez in 1795.

So what he claims in his 1835 Preface is true. Encouraged by the success of *Spain and Portugal* in 1834, he rummaged through his Papers, found and read through the 'very slight notes of this Excursion' jotted down as he travelled in 1794, and then, artist and poet that he was, 'invoked the powers of memory and up rose the whole series of recollections', inextricably mingled with fantasy and over half a century's reading of other people's travel-books and memoirs.

As so often, the *unpublished* manuscript biography of his first biographer, Cyrus Redding, is illuminating and partly correct. This version was suppressed and bought up by Beckford's daughter, the Duchess of Hamilton, which accounts for the disappointing nature of the much later authorised and printed version. Redding, who knew Beckford in Bath at the time he was writing his *Excursion* says: 'He stated that this fragment was put together from a few scanty notes and entirely worked out from memory in his seventy-fourth year. He possessed other notes but said he was too indolent to invoke the powers of memory on their behalf and he feared further that in the present day they might have lost their interest. The excursion to Alcobaça and Batalha is all therefore of which the world is likely to hear anything in its regard and this is the more to be lamented from the style being so novel and the subjects treated of having been inaccessible to other travellers'.[7] The other alleged notes have disappeared, but it sounds as if they dealt more with politics (in which Beckford was not too interested), or with scandalous material about personages in Portugal too long dead to be interesting to the British public.

Most importantly, the 1794 Journal shows that in Beckford's expedition there was no Twelfth Day, when he allegedly met at the Royal Palace of Queluz the Prince Regent (as he was called a little later) and his wife the notorious Carlota Joaquina, afterwards Queen. They could not have received him in the way he describes because he was not officially presented at their Court until the next year. The *Excursion* makes out that by Royal command he accompanied the Prior of St. Vincent and the Grand Prior of Aviz on an official mission to the monasteries. But the Journal shows that St. Vincent did not accompany them; and we know that dear old Aviz was quite unimportant, owing his sinecure to his bastard relationship to the 'old' Marquis of Marialva (the father of Beckford's friend of 1787). Furthermore, Aviz left Beckford for Lisbon on the Tenth Day, so could not, as it were, have slipped his friend into the Palace by the back door. Beckford's only companions at this stage were his personal physician Ehrhart, a suspect liberal of Alsatian birth, and Franchi, the choirboy friend of 1787.

Alas, one of the major purposes of the *Excursion* was to make the English Establishment and public of 1835 believe that Beckford, still *hors de société* but still thirsting for the peerage revoked in 1784, had been persona grata in Court circles abroad, a person of importance and good reputation, even perhaps able to sway events by backstairs influence.

Whibley, writing in 1900 (only sixty-five years after Beckford's publication), falls nicely into this cleverly prepared trap. Commenting on Beckford's day at Queluz, he concludes: 'His progress through Portugal, then, was an unbroken glory. With his French cook to aid, he captivated the country; the Court, the Nobles, and the Church paid him extravagant honour; and he carried back to England a memory which, though merged in imagination, still flattered his vanity after fifty years.' Lockhart, on the cooked-up evidence of *Spain and Portugal*, comes to the same conclusion: 'England's wealthiest son performs his travels, of course, in a style of great external splendour. . . courts and palaces, as well as convents and churches and galleries of all sorts, fly open at his approach: he is caressed in every capital – he is *fêté* in every chateau.'

It is fascinating how Beckford builds on half-truths and manipulates facts. For example, in his account of his alleged interview at Queluz with the Prince, he writes of the latter 'honouring me again with those affable expressions of regard which his excellent heart never failed to dictate.' He was indeed on these cordial surface terms after presentation a year later, as is shown by a touching letter in Portuguese from his devoted friend Marialva, the favourite courtier of the Portuguese Royal Family and father of the 'young' Marquis of Marialva mentioned by Beckford at Queluz. Marialva writes to Beckford back in England in 1796: 'My beloved friend,. . . never a Packet arrives without the Prince asking me at once, "Has good news of Beckford come?" And I thank him heartily on your behalf for his enquiry, and show him the letter you have sent me, which he reads thoughtfully, rejoicing in your expressions about him; and sometimes he has said to me: 'He is your friend, but he is mine too'." '[8]

By the way, the alleged interview with Prince João in 1794 should not be confused with the 1787 meeting with the then heir, his elder brother the Prince of Brazil, recorded as a highlight in *Spain and Portugal*. I have shown in *England's Wealthiest Son* that there is no reason to suppose that this is not a true account.

Here I must make a historical diversion to illuminate some interesting passages in the *Excursion*. The elder Prince died of smallpox in 1788 and was succeeded as heir by Prince João; his death was partly caused by the religious scruples of his mother, Maria I, who forbade vaccination. This was the origin of the rumour that he had been allowed to die because of his liberal political views, which made him suspect to the largely reactionary nobility. In any event the Queen, prone to a strong sense of guilt, would have felt herself to blame for his death. In the same year she lost through death her main pillar of moral support and comfort, her Confessor, the comparitively moderate Archbishop de S. Caetano. She had already felt keenly the loss of her husband in 1786. The final factors in her mental collapse, which led to permanent madness from 1791, were fears engendered in Court circles by the French Revolution and the inexorable pressure of her new Confessor the Bishop of Algarve, whom Beckford in an interesting footnote to Letter XXXIII of *Portugal* rightly calls a 'fanatical, interested priest'.

As Beckford shows in the Twelfth Day of the *Excursion*, the pressure on her by the nobility, abetted by her new Confessor, centred on their efforts to secure the full rehabilitation of, and restoration of property to, the heirs of the Duke of Aveiro and Marquis of Tavora. These and some of their relations were brutally executed in public in 1759 by the dictator Pombal for their alleged part in a plot to murder Jose I, father of Maria I. The latter succeeded her father, to whose memory she was piously devoted, in 1777; ever since then the nobles had been trying to get all members of these two families rehabilitated. Maria wished to protect the memory of her father, particularly since his scandalous love life was involved in the attempt on him (the young Marchioness of Tavora was his mistress). Ten years after her succession the strain was already too much for her. Beckford was told this by Marialva, and confided it to his Journal on 22 October 1787: '[Marialva] told me in the strictest confidence that the Queen had thoughts of retiring from government, that she was worn out with the intrigues of the Court and sick of her existence.'

This indicates that when Beckford brings in Portuguese politics he has something worthwhile to say, particularly since he knew or had met most of the participants, and learnt much through the Marialvas. So there is no need to doubt in the Twelfth Day of the *Excursion* his description of one of the Queen's recurrent nightmares: 'In a paroxysm of mental agony she kept crying out for mercy, imagining that in the midst of a raging flame which enveloped the whole chamber she beheld her father's image a calcined mass of cinder – a statue in form like that [to him] in the Terreiro do Paço, but in colour black and horrible – erected on a pedestal of molten iron, which a crowd of ghastly phantoms – she named them, I shall not – were in the act of dragging down.

This vision haunts her by night and by day.' The book ends with her agonising wail '*Ai Jesous! Ai Jesous!*', which echoes in the reader's ear. Her vision reflects her fear that, by agreeing to rehabilitate the Tavoras, she is guilty of destroying the honour and tarnishing the memory of her father. The early Romantics were good at describing these states of mind, which preoccupied them. So in the Seventh Day we find an acute account of the onset and progress of mental unbalance and decay, brought on by the shock of events. Beckford gives the history of the mad monk at Batalha, once a gay young nobleman, relative of the accused Duke of Aveiro, and therefore imprisoned with him (after a ball, as Beckford says); years later he was released. Here is part of the story of his progressive loss of interest in the world until he paced the moonlit gardens of Batalha prophesying, in between the nightingale's song, Judgement and Woe upon Portugal: 'in the course of years and events, the slender lovely youth now become a wasted careworn man, emerged [from prison] to sorrow and loneliness. The blood of his dearest relatives seemed sprinkled upon every object that met his eyes; he never passed Belem without fancying he beheld, as in a sort of frightful dream, the scaffold, the wheels on which those he best loved had expired in torture . . . he felt benumbed and paralysed; the world, the court, had no charms for him; there was for him no longer warmth in the sun or smiles on the human countenance; a stranger to love or fear or any interest on this side the grave, he gave up his entire soul to prayer.' This story could be true. Some of the principal accused were arrested by cavalry who surrounded their homes on their return from a ball given by the English Factory. And young Tavora, amongst others, was also at a ball at Aveiro's house during the attempt on the King's life.

No one would guess from the light-heartedness of the *Excursion* (gay, that is to say, apart from the two examples just given, and his occasional ranting about the French Revolution) that Beckford at this time, and probably often later, feared insanity – knowing that he had a frantic temper, that his strange family was 'accursed' and that his grandfather had committed murder. Yet shortly after his return from the monasteries, he composed in French the following soliloquy at Monserrate, his *quinta* near Cintra: 'Great talents are gifts for which often we pay much more dearly than they are worth. They are associated with such great sensibility that it is almost impossible to control. And yet we glory in this divine fire which may at any moment annihilate us and destroy all our happiness! Voltaire died mad, and the derangement of Rousseau's mind in his last years approached insanity. Thus, what we prize most highly when we only know its fine aspect, becomes the object of our aversion when we see its dark side . . . . Our bearing is much affected by temperance; we cannot pay this too much attention when vexed. A little bile, a slight difficulty darkens the imagination and stirs the distressing passions of pride, hatred and revenge.'[9]

This background of self-distrust, religious despair, anxiety and pessimism, which spread into every aspect of his life, makes all the more remarkable his achievement in writing the gay *Excursion* when so old. To the end there was a certain unexpected verve, buoyancy and toughness in this spoiled child. He expresses this in a letter in French announcing the financial coup of the sale of his beloved birthplace and home for sixty-two years – Fonthill: 'They flattered themselves that I had foundered, but they are deucedly mistaken
"Strong I breast the waves".'[10]

In fact, in the *Excursion* there is only one passage in which he hints at the regret, self-reproach and sense of lost opportunity which dogged his life and which were already closing in on him during that carefree summer of 1794: 'Throwing myself on the solid ground, I kept intensely poring over the stream, lost and absorbed in the train of interesting yet melancholy recollections which all that had occurred to me since I first entered this fair realm of Portugal was so well calculated to excite. I thought (alas! how vainly now!) of offers I had slighted with so much levity; of opportunities which, had they been grasped with a decided hand, might have led to happy results and stemmed a torrent of evils.' But having said this, he at once throws us off the scent by commenting: 'Since that period, the germ of destructiveness, which might then have been trodden down, has risen into a tree fraught with poisons, darkening the wholesome light and receiving nourishment, through all its inumerably varied fibres, from the lowest depths of hell.' (Eighth Day).

But Redding fastens on to this reverie, realising that it has a personal rather than a political significance. In a comment suppressed by the Duchess of Hamilton he adds that it was 'written under the influence of that impatient feeling, with which at times he was possessed, of his not having done enough in the way of acquirement, of his having thrown away his times and opportunities.' In a manuscript which he hoped to publish shortly after Beckford's death, Redding could not hint at more than this. But we may fairly suggest that, unconsciously or otherwise, Beckford is supplying a metaphor for the development of his inner life since 1787, as I have explained in *England's Wealthiest Son.*[11]

We have seen that he was well acquainted with the internal politics of Portugal. Is he fair in his description of the two monasteries? Allowing for his exaggeration to produce literary effect and to trumpet his alleged importance, and discounting his fervid imagination, he does at least bring out the essential difference between the two establishments. We can check his impressions against the sober account of Murphy, who stayed in each monastery much longer than Beckford and only five years before, in 1789. At Alcobaça he found about 300 people, including servants 'living in a splendid manner'. Its royal founder had endowed it with so much land that it was 'one of the richest and most magnificent institutions of the kind not only in Portugal but in Europe'. Even before Murphy's time its privileges had been curtailed and the size of its revenue criticised 'from an idea that wealth promotes feasting more than praying.' But he writes that 'during a residence here of near three weeks, I could perceive no just grounds for such remarks; on the contrary, I found the greatest temperance and decorum, blended with hospitality and cheerfulness, prevail in every part. . . . Those who declaim against their opulence, would do well to enquire whether there be a nobleman or gentleman in Europe, possessed of a revenue equal to that of this Monastery, who diffuses so many blessings among his fellow-beings as the Fathers of Alcobaça.'

Like Beckford, who was interested in such things, Murphy observes that their tenants were well cared for. He adds other useful details – they maintained and educated many local youths and looked after the poor 'so that hundreds of indigent people are constantly fed at their gates'. On the great kitchen which so fascinated Beckford, Murphy is almost epigrammatic: 'Notwithstanding the magnitude of this apartment, there is not an inch of it unoccupied from morning till night; for all the industry of the Convent is concentrated in it.'[12]

Murphy describes the simple and comparatively frugal life at Batalha, whose monks distributed to the poor a great part of their daily allowance. He analyses the occupations of the fifty-eight clerical and lay members of the establishment. Fourteen servants sounds to us a lot, but they include a shepherd, hogherd, baker, shoemaker, laundress and muleteers – a self-supporting establishment giving useful employment locally.

But there is a certain ambiguity if not discrepancy in Murphy's comments on the integrity of the monks and their way of life in both communities. It is therefore interesting to find that, although an Irish Catholic of humble birth, in a suppressed extract of his travel-journal he writes of Batalha: 'The mass-friars have nothing to do but to eat and drink, saunter about or sleep. The prior is a plain homely kind of man, distinguished from the rest only by a small black cap and the priviledge of wearing a dirty face. What a pity it is to see so many stout fellows leading a life of indolence and sloth, that might be of service in cultivating the land, in feeding the poor and enriching or defending their country.'[13] Beckford too is ambivalent in his attitude towards monastic goings-on, so that Lockhart wrongly concludes that 'from a thousand passing sneers, we may doubt that he has any religion at all.'

In the end, when considering Beckford as a travel-writer, we have to remember that, despite his detailed eye as a sarcastic observer, he wilfully prefers Illusion and Dream to reality, like so many Romantics. As he approaches Batalha on the Eighth Day, this is how he tries to see it: 'in appearance it was not merely a church or a palace I was looking at, but some fair city of romance, such as an imagination glowing with the fancies of Ariosto might have pictured to itself under the illusion of a dream. Keeping my eyes fixed on a prospect which I tried to persuade myself partook less of the real than the visionary. . .'

What is his settled view of Portugal? Here too there is apparent ambiguity. Out there he is often exasperated by 'this fag-end of Europe', as he calls it in a letter in 1794. Yet a few months later in his 1794 Journal he speaks charmingly of it in a much quoted entry which he included (slightly altered) in the Fourth Day of the *Excursion:* 'How often, contrasting my quiet situation with the horrid disturbed state of almost every part of Europe, did I bless the hour when my steps were directed to Portugal. I looked round with complacency on a roof which sheltered no politician, on tables [upon] which perhaps no newspaper had ever lain, on neat white pillows which had never propped up the heads of financiers and schemers.' Admittedly this is a hit at his lifelong enemy, our Prime Minister Pitt, and at City merchants among whom Alderman Beckford was once numbered. There is also the unspoken thought that the Portuguese aristocracy and rich men enjoy a privileged position under the protection of 'the benign power of royal proclamations, with their paternal advice to people of the lower orders to leave untroubled the repose of the heroes of the upper classes'(as he wrote ironically later on). But one knows what he means when he speaks thus of the blessed peace and simplicity of rural Portugal, even though she was at war with revolutionary France.

It is of this rural, flower-strewn beauty that he is sometimes reminded years later, on a fine summer day at Fonthill. Once, for example, he walks in his grounds with Bezerra, his friend since 1787, now an important ambassador and later acting Prime Minister: 'The weather is favourable for walking and the walks are divinely beautiful – roses everywhere, *azareiri* covered with flowers, cloud-mountains in the air gilded by the rays of the sun, the most brilliant effects of chiaroscuro, stranger than I ever before remember having seen, and due to the recent drought. I wish you were here to see these picturesque mists and, above all, to breathe the scent of Cintra and Collares, which makes poor Bezerra weep and fills him with the tenderest *saudades*'. Three weeks later, during the same marvellous summer of 1810, he writes 'Today there are clouds above the Tower and the hill, and a real threat of rain – sweet, poetic, melancholy weather that recalls languid memories of Cintra and Monserrate'. Because he saw scenery, buildings and people with the eye of an artist, because he had the retentive visual memory of the trained art connoisseur, and because he saw his past with the nostaglia of a poet, he could recreate at the age of seventy-four what he had experienced forty years earlier. Of past memories (in which he constantly lived) 'memories of Portugal will always be the memories nearest to my heart', he writes in 1812.

At the time of the Convention of Cintra in 1808 he completely identified himself in imagination with the Portuguese, over whose prone bodies the two great military Occupying Powers of England and France negotiated: 'O poor, beloved Portugal, my own true country, how I pity you!'[14]

So when he wrote the *Excursion,* these ever-present memories of Portugal bubble up irrepressibly, as we can tell from a phrase in his daughter's letter, written in French to her husband the Duke of Hamilton a few weeks after the book's publication. She says 'I really *haven't the strength* to see him [Beckford] for hours of *discours* on Alcobaça'[15]

In conclusion, what did he expect of readers and reviewers on the appearance of his last book to be published during his lifetime? Despite the glowing and perceptive thirty-page analysis by Lockhart of *Spain and Portugal*, the latter had a mixed reception amongst reviewers and the *Edinburgh Review* ignored it despite Disraeli's pressing offer to notice it for them. Beckford was one of the most unpopular men in England. People were ready to judge his writings by his reputation, and to read into them what they thought they knew of his character.

This philistine and hostile attitude to his aestheticism is wittily described by him in a mock-review he drafted in anticipation of the criticism he expected of *Spain and Portugal*. All that he says could equally well be applied by such people to the *Excursion* and so is worth printing here:

'This publication, we may venture to affirm, will not add to the *reputation* of the author of V— if the authorship of that wild orientalist extravaganza can be said to confer any. It would have been as well for the public as for the author had these flimsy letters remained in the portfolio . . . for the flowery, inflated prose of these letters or epistles or whatever anybody may please to call them is calculated to disgust rather than attract readers of taste and lovers of a purer and less effeminate style of composition.

'What may have awakened smiles of approbation [for] a youthful adventurer in literature as holding out something of promise, must be refused the veteran who, in the full maturity of years, for reasons we have as yet to discover, has been emboldened, as he tells us, to put them forth after having lain dormant for so long, and never could the two doggerel verses said to have been scribbled on a tombstone be better applied than upon this occasion:

Lie still if you're wise,
You'll be d—d if you rise.

To enter into any detail of the contents of these ultra picturesque letters is scarcely worthwhile, but it is our duty to caution those who might feel disposed to open these volumes. Let it suffice to make mention that they contain scarcely one grain of information or one sentiment indicative of a well-regulated mind or manly intellect.'[16]

Reader, beware!

BOYD ALEXANDER
October, 1971

Notes to Introduction

1. Quotations from Whibley are from his essay on Beckford in *Pageantry of Life*, 1st. ed., 1900.
2. Quotations from Rose Macaulay are from her essay on Beckford in *They Went to Portugal*, 1946.
3. Quotations from Lockhart are from his review of *Italy, Spain and Portugal* in *Quarterly Review*, Vol. 51, pp. 428–30.
4. Elton: *Survey of English Literature, 1780–1830*, (1912), I. 206.
5. Daiches: *Critical History of English Literature*, 1960, II. 741.
6. Catalogue of Exhibition for Bicentenary of Beckford's Birth, Yale University Library, 1960: Appendix 2.
7. Redding: MS *Memoirs of William Beckford*, 1846 (in Hamilton Papers), II. 7.
8. See my *England's Wealthiest Son*, 1962, p. 133.
9. Ditto, pp. 242–3.
10. See my *Life at Fonthill*, 1957, p. 341, where there is a misprint in the Latin tag (which I have translated here)
11. *England's Wealthiest Son*, pp. 136 – 7. Not in the 1794 Diary, but seems genuine for that period
12. James Murphy: *Travels in Portugal . . . in 1789 and 1790* (1795), pp. 100 –101, 93. For my next para on Batalha, see his pp. 45–6
13. W. H. Harrison: *Tourist in Portugal*, 1839, pp. 142–3
14. These last five quotations are from *Life at Fonthill*, pp. 311, 91, 94, 125, 83 (all originally in Italian)
15. Unpublished letter of 28 July 1835, in Hamilton Papers
16. Printed in Oliver: *Life of William Beckford*, 1932, pp. 307–8, without date; but actually dated 22 January 1834

The above notes are kept to a minimum, but all sources quoted are acknowledged in them. As will be seen, I have quoted briefly from two fine modern critics, the late Rose Macaulay (published by Cape) and Professor Daiches (Secker & Warburg), to whose publishers I am grateful. Biographical details of some people in the *Excursion* are in my *Journal of William Beckford in Portugal and Spain, 1787–88*, (1954), and of Dr. Ehrhart in *Life at Fonthill*. Useful titles, notes and a map are in Parreaux' French translation of the *Excursion*, Paris and Lisbon, 1956 (in which he follows the text, etc., of the second edition of 1840).

Appendix
Beckford's 1794 Journal

[Editor's note: Pointed brackets indicate an editorial insertion; when there are no words inside, a word or phrase is illegible in the manuscript. Trifling abbreviations have been expanded, and Beckford's punctuation, spelling of proper names and grammatical errors altered where necessary for clarity. His later alterations have been ignored. Reproduced with permission of Hamilton & Kinneil Estates.]

Monday 2 June, 1794 <First Day>
One of the most glowing evening suns I ever beheld was throwing away its interesting beams upon the dull unpicturesque environs of Lisbon when I set off for Tojal, a *quinta* under the dominion of my friend the Prior of St. Vincent's. This was to be our first stage on the route of Alcobaça. The Grand Prior of Aviz accompanied me in my large English chaise, which from its size and the number of trunks and bundles stowed about it gave the gaping inhabitants of Lisbon a good pretext for calling it a packet <boat> upon four wheels. In this huge machine we were drawn by six mules not without difficulty over the rough < > pavements of the road to Bemfica.

Beyond this village a shady lane overhung by elms brought us to an open space before the Convent of Nossa Senhora de Luz. This pile of buildings, which appears to have been considerable, was much shattered by the earthquake. Not containing any object worth examination, we passed on to Lumiar thro' intricate paved roads between hedges of laurel, pomegranate and aloe, the stalks in them sprouting up to the height of ten or twelve feet in the shape and colour of asparagus.

Lumiar contains a *quinta* belonging to the Marquis of Angeja, upon which immense sums have been lavished for the wise purpose of pebbling alleys in quaint mosaic patterns, red, black and blue; building gigantic reservoirs for gold and silver fish; painting their smooth plastered sides with divers flaming colours; and cutting a steep hill into a succession of stiff terraces for the sole pretext, one would think, of establishing flights of awkward narrow marble steps to communicate one with another.

The outward appearance of the houses in this village is tolerably neat, the walls whitewashed, and vine arbours projecting before every door; but within, all kinds of filth is heaped up in profusion, and every sort of vermin encouraged. The country appears extremely populous; vast numbers of peasants, as sunburnt and nearly as lightly-clothed as the natives of Otaheite, were passing on mules and in carts in busy confusion.

The road from Lumiar to Loures is constructed along a valley highly cultivated and bounded by lofty hills, variegated by fields of grain and wild shrubby pastures. The soft air of the evening was delightful.

It grew dark when we passed thro' the village of Tojal, and crossing a bridge over the River Trancaõ, entered the woody domain of the monks of St. Vincent by a handsome stone gateway surmounted by a cross. Here we found ourselves in a thick grove of orange trees. Lights glimmered in the windows of the house, which seemed to rise out, and directed us to it. Our reception was truly hospitable and splendid. The instructive gaiety and cheerful politeness of our host the Prior were never more conspicuous.

After a supper infinitely more copious and delicate than we required, I retired to a cool pleasant apartment spread with Persian carpets and decorated with a good picture of my beloved Saint Anthony; and slept till the sunbeams, entering my window (*Tuesday June 3rd*) summoned me to enjoy the fresh morning breeze blowing over a woody valley.

<Tuesday, 3 June: Second Day>
After breakfast we walked amongst well-cultivated vegetables, fields of Indian wheat, and the most extensive orchards of orange,

apricot and other fruit trees I ever beheld. Every inch of ground within the enclosure – and I should imagine not less than two hundred acres are surrounded by the wall – is turned to the most advantageous account. The oranges alone produce from seven to eight thousand cruzados a year. A very active intelligent lay brother has the management of this fortunate spot, and is continually extending it over the bare hills in the neighbourhood, many of which are comprised within the domain of the Fathers. They have a never failing command of water, and pour down fertility at pleasure over their possessions.

The river Trancaô which runs through the garden is almost diminished to a brook at this season, but this brook is clear and flows pretty rapidly. The rocky edges, worn into picturesque irregular shapes by winter torrents, bloom at this season with the rose-coloured flowers of the oleander. Their appearance was strikingly beautiful; many of these shrubs had attained the height of fifteen or sixteen feet.

But one of the grandest objects of the vegetable world which ever met my sight is a bay tree situated in the thickest part of the wood of orange trees, above which it towers majestically, clothed with luxuriant boughs that glisten with health and vigour. It consists of about thirty stems, none less than two feet and some thirty-eight inches in diameter, springing from one root, and rising to the height of sixty-four feet. I loitered away the sultry hour of midday most pleasantly under its deep fragrant shade.

The Prior had ordered a fishing party for my amusement, but I cannot bring myself to be amused with these displays of human tyranny. I turned with disgust and sorrow from the poor unfortunate animals rudely thrown upon a bare sandy bank and gasping for life. We children of Adam should be justly punished were some gigantic inhabitants of another planet permitted by the Great Disposer of all things to fish us out of our element into some other where our lungs would be useless and we should try to breathe in vain. Courtesy obliged both the Grand Prior and myself and Dr. Ehrhart to remain much longer than we liked on the banks of the river witnessing the agonies of the expiring fish.

About two o'clock we returned home thro' shady alleys of bay and orange, divided by canes mantled with vines, which promised, like every plant in this happy enclosure, an abundant produce. The nightingales were singing in the recesses of the woods impenetrable to the sun, and at the same time, I am sorry to add, frogs were croaking a deep thorough-bass to this enchanting melody.

We dined late for the sake of devouring the fruits of our fishery, prepared in a particular manner by the fishermen themselves. It was a sort of *matelotte*, well made and seasoned, but the fish were muddy. I don't remember to have seen the same species in England; they call them *boga*. Dr. Ehrhart perhaps may know their scientific appellation and I will ask him.

In the cool of the evening we drove to the village of Tojal, where the Patriarch has a large mansion containing nothing in the least remarkable except a vestibule with a tribune looking into a church. The walls of this apartment are lined with a variety of Italian marbles mixed with some fine specimens, the produce of Spain and Portugal; they are dispersed in panels and ornamented with gilt bronze in a tolerable style. The garden corresponds in formal dismality with the Palace. I was glad to escape from it and return to the orange thickets of Tojal, where I walked till almost midnight, listening to the nightingales who had happily shamed the frogs to silence.

Wednesday, June 4th <Third Day>
The heat made me completely lazy, and the sight and example of the Grand Prior, who is the very soul of laziness, increased this disposition to such a degree that I could do nothing but read in an idle, desultory manner. At dinner the lively instructive conversation of the Prior of St. Vincent's – by far the most conversable person I have met with in this country – revived my spirits. We passed the evening in rambling about his vast gardens and admiring the manner in which they are watered and cultivated.

Thursday, June 5th <Fourth Day>
I was awakened out of a sound refreshing sleep at half past four much against my inclination, so felt but ill-disposed to enjoy the freshness of morning, the clear light of the rising sun and other delights which poets and early risers talk of. I saw no appearance

of dew; there was no vapour, no morning mist lingering in the valley all was hard and dry.

By the time we had breakfasted and the carriages were got ready, clouds began to appear to my utter surprise, and gathering rapidly, overspread almost the whole horizon. Under this cool canopy which I suspect to have been spread over the face of the heavens by particular desire of St. Anthony, we had the pleasure of travelling. Above, everything was as we could wish; but below, the road was abominably uneven and threatened every instant to lay my heavy carriage with all its glories in the dust.

We passed <Granja de> Alpriate, a chateau of the Duke of Lafoes, a good deal in the French style. It stands in a valley which would be pleasant if any other trees than the pale leaden-coloured olive happened to predominate. After jolting and jumbling along for about a league, we emerged from this chaos of ruts and broken sandbanks into the great highway which leads to the Caldas through Alhandra, Povos and Villa Franca. These places which are neither small nor unpopulous, are not unpleasantly situated on the banks of the Tagus, and have *quintas*, palaces and fidalgos as well as their betters. The face of the country is rather flat. The breadth of the river and its low shoals striped with ditches full of water for the purposes of irrigation recalled to my mind the scenery of the worst parts of Holland and the environs of Antwerp.

As Her Most Faithful Majesty and the Royal Family frequently resort to the Caldas for the purpose of steeping their crazy limbs in its salubrious waters, this road is handsomely formed and kept in tolerable repair; and at every league pedestals with vases upon them are erected, and in some places fountains with inscriptions setting forth that in such a year and under the administration of such and such personages they were ordered to be made. Some spell or other seems to prevent the finishing of anything in Portugal. Don't imagine therefore that half these fountains or league stones are completed. The vase lies unerected in several places, by its pedestal; upon the greatest part of which the number, still unengraved, is carelessly scribbled in black paint. I thought this instance of sluggishness and indifference to every object of use or ornament strongly characteristic of this nation of slaves and slovens.

However, thanks to the goodness of soil and climate and that indulgent Providence which takes compassion of the poor in spirit, they will have bread to eat. The country between Villa Franca and Carregado exhibits an appearance of great plenty – Turkish corn in abundance, fine barley and immense fields of black Sicilian wheat, the ears bending to the ground with their weight.

Near Carregado, where we abandoned the high road in order to reach Cadafaiz – another domain under the government of our hospitable friend the Prior of St. Vincent's – the harvest was gathering in. Just as we left the last-mentioned village, the sun shone forth and illuminated one of the most cheerful landscapes I ever beheld. We were surrounded by an endless succession of lofty hills, the highest about 150 *toises*, all cultivated to their very summits, and most picturesquely varied by chestnut copses and ledges of rock peeping out of wild shrubberies formed by broom, cistus of various kinds, and heaths of the liveliest green. A clear river flows between these agreeable little mountains, bordered by thick tufts of poplar and willows, with here and there a cypress or pine spiring out of their bosoms. I readily excused the extreme badness of the road for the sake of the pleasant rural spots thro' which it led, and was almost sorry to arrive about noon at the end of our day's journey.

We found ourselves in a most comfortable farm house perfectly clean and cheerful, the floors neatly matted, the tables covered with the finest white linen, and Bohemian caraffes filled with carnations. A good-natured lay brother was bustling about and preparing everything for our comfort and convenience under the good-natured intelligent eye of our amiable host. The windows of the snug apartment allotted to me commanded the view of a boundless vineyard in full luxuriant leaf, divided by long walks, well kept and weeded. From this immense sea of green leaves, rose a number of plum, pear, peach and apricot trees covered with fruit. Not a worm or insect seemed to have preyed upon their healthy foliage. Beyond this rich scene of plenty and cultivation, the hills I have mentioned before swell into the most picturesque forms and completely enclose this calm retirement. Vast spaces of wild mountain pasture divide the cornfields and vineyards and still retain the verdure of spring.

These are the spots I peculiarly delight in, where I seem to breathe with greater freedom, and which the goats and sheep, whose bells I heard tinkling at a distance, love not better than I. How often, contrasting my quiet situation with the horrid disturbed state of almost every part of Europe, did I bless the hour when my steps were directed to Portugal. I looked round with complacency on a roof which sheltered no politician, on tables <upon> which perhaps no newspaper had ever lain, on neat white pillows which had never propped up the heads of financiers and schemers. The air was genially warm, and every breeze wafted the perfume of thyme, wild roses and honeysuckle from the hills.

Monday, 9th June <Alcobaça>
Cloister built by D<om> Diniz. Fountain before <the> refectory, an immense square of seventy or eighty feet; linen foul and greasy. Chapter House dismal; painted glass windows – < > of abbots and their chairs as ugly and horned as that in which Satan is represented to sit at the Sabbath; the walls covered with sepulchral inscriptions to the memory of the knights slain in the Battle of Aljubarota. This evening a sleek friar with wanton eyes accompanied Franchi on the Jew's harp; I hear him twanging away at this moment.

Wednesday, June 11 <Ninth Day>
From Alcobaça to Pederneira on the edge of a clear river full to the brim; ample beds of flag flowers. <The> Grand Prior in agonies of fear upon passing a bridge without parapets – agonies which all my exhortations for having faith in St. Anthony could not subdue – so out he trundled into all the dust, filth and carrion of the road. Vast plain in a high state of cultivation belonging to the Convent, as well as the whole country far and wide. Peasants neither meagre, unhealthy or ragged, which gives me reason to hope they are not oppressed. A long string of female peasants passing the hills carrying presents to Nossa Senhora de Nazarè. Vast woods of pine; warm genial fragrant breezes.

About one o'clock arrive at Pederneira, a house belonging to the monks, where we dined upon excellent fish. Ehrhart gobbled fish and roast pig indiscriminately, to the utter scandal of the monk who accompanied us and attendant lay brother. Sea view beautiful. The sanctuary of Nazarè appears mean and pitiful.

Behind the church grows the *papaver corniculatum* in great abundance; strong healthy yellow flowers. Between Pederneira and Caldas, yellow sweet-scented lupins in abundance. I was assured upon the faith of a Jesuit priest, who is a botanist, that a scarlet lupin, decidedly scarlet, was gathered by him a spring or two ago, believe that who will.

Drag heavily thro' sand. At a distance a Moorish castle standing proudly on an insulated eminence presenting a grand mass; it bears a grand name, Alfeizeraõ; arrive in the night.

Thursday, June 12 <Tenth Day>
Morning cloudy and pleasant. I have been cheated at a swinging rate by one of those harpies called *provedores*, who under the mask of administering justice, superintending hospitals, etc. divert every little rill of Royal beneficence into their own pockets. This knave was so accustomed to the sweets of monopolies that he bought up half the fowls, turkeys and provisions in the place, and then dealt them out for me and my numerous train at his own price. I refused seeing this cormorant, having been startled at his bill – which was lucky, as I am told he joins insolence to knavery.

We saw Obidos with its towers and battlemented walls rising above a forest of pines; to the left a long line of aqueduct connecting it with the neighbouring hills. The hills, being clothed with a thick vegetation of dwarf ilex, myrtles, etc., at a distance look as beautifully green as if covered with turf.

Dine at Cercal, a pleasant situation at the foot of shrubby hills. At the entrance of the village an irregular sloping lawn, bounded by enclosures with green hedges, forming shady lanes filled with a variety of shrubs in blossom. Flock of turkeys and their young busily employed in picking up emmets' eggs and destroying the hopes of many a family of this species. I trod forth the perfume of a thousand aromatic herbs < >. It was not oppressively hot; the sky of a pale tender blue, indescribably serene and beautiful. To breathe the soft air of this climate is no small luxury. It seems to diffuse new life into every vein, and if to these gifts of nature the blessings of a free government and the refinements of art were added, it would require more philosophy than I am master of not to murmur blasphemously at the shortness of our existence.

Our road in the evening lay between sandy mountains partially covered by bushes of rosemary and lavender. The sun sunk behind the chain of hills which form the coast of the sea just as we reached a *quinta* belonging to Forjaz, at present Governor of Madeira, and gave place to the moon. As we approached the rich cultivated plains framed in by the hills round Cadafaiz, we heard the country people, men, women and children, singing hymns to St. Anthony as they returned home from reaping. A faint breeze just ruffled the wavy surface of their cornfields.

At Carregado I took leave of the Grand Prior who proceeded straight to Lisbon; and getting on horseback <I> once more left the high road to take that of Cadafaiz. The hills which surround this retired spot were blazing with fires; I counted twenty-two shining bright amongst the olive trees as I proceeded slowly, enjoying my moonlight reveries. The hospitable Prior of St. Vincent's was waiting my arrival. I feasted upon fine ripe cherries, and forgot that it was late, and that I was fatigued, in the conversation of our host.

Friday, 13th June <Eleventh Day>
I shook off laziness manfully, and tho' it was boiling hot, set off with the Prior and his attendents for the Franciscan Convent, whose pious inhabitants were trimming all their lamps, lighting all their tapers and making every preparation in their power to celebrate the festival of St. Anthony. The verdure I so much admired upon first seeing Cadafaiz a week ago is withering apace, the fields already reaped present dreary wastes of stubble, and the whole landscape changed much for the worse.

We found a vast concourse of people upon the summit of the mountain, in general very comfortably clad – the corps of beggars excepted, who never fail attending upon these occasions and setting forth their tatters and their infirmities to the best advantage. Perfect good humour and good order seemed to prevail. I heard no swearing, ranting or squabbling. I saw no guzzling or wallowing. Everyone seemed penetrated with the solemn business of the day and to make their offerings at the altar of St. Anthony with unaffected devotion.

It was not without difficulty we made our way through the crowd to the church door where we waited till a procession of young lads, dressed in an odd oriental style probably in fashion when the Moors ruled Portugal, had entered. Several of these devotees bore fat lambs on their shoulders, who had been pampered, washed and bedecked with ribbons for the occasion; others, sacks of flour; the best dressed and the best looking carried on a sort of sledge ornamented with flowers, a huge lump of wax in the shape of a candle as thick as a moderate-sized garden roller in England, and flourished over with various devices, amongst which the Saint's cypher in gold and silver wire shone conspicuous.

Alcobaça and Batalha

FIRST DAY
Supreme command given to two distinguished Prelates to visit the
Monasteries of Alcobaça and Batalha, and a royal wish expressed
that the Author should accompany them.—Preparations in high
style for the Journey.—The general Rendezvous.—Departure.—
Nossa Senhora de Luz.—Lumiares.—Domain of the Monks of
St. Vincent.—Reception there.

3rd June, 1794.

The Prince Regent of Portugal, for reasons with which I was
never entirely acquainted, took it into his royal head, one fair
morning, to desire I would pay a visit to the monasteries of
Alcobaça and Batalha, and to name my intimate and particular
friends, the Grand Prior of Aviz, and the Prior of St. Vincent's,
as my conductors and companions. Nothing could be more
gracious, and, in many respects, more agreeable; still, just at this
moment, having what I thought much pleasanter engagements
nearer home, I cannot pretend that I felt so much enchanted as
I ought to have been.

Upon communicating the supreme command to the two
prelates, they discovered not the smallest token of surprise; it
seemed they were fully prepared for it. The Grand Prior observed
that the weather was dreadfully hot, and the roads execrable:
the other prelate appeared more animated, and quite ready for
the expedition. I thought I detected in one corner of his lively,
intelligent eye, a sparkle of hope that, when returned from his
little cruise of observation, the remarks it was likely enough to
inspire might lead to more intimate conferences at Queluz, and
bring him into more frequent collision with royalty.

As my right reverend companions had arranged not to renounce one atom of their habitual comforts and conveniences, and to take with them their confidential acolytes and secretaries, as well as some of their favourite quadrupeds, we had in the train of the latter-mentioned animals a rare rabble of grooms, ferradors, and mule-drivers. To these, my usual followers being added, we formed altogether a caravan which, camels and dromedaries excepted, would have cut no despicable figure even on the route of Mecca or Mesched-Ali!

The rallying point, the general rendezvous for the whole of this heterogeneous assemblage, was my quinta of San José, commanding in full prospect the entrance of the Tagus, crowded with vessels arriving from every country under the heavens, messengers of joy to some, of sorrow to others, but all with expanded sails equally brightening in the beams of the cheerful sun, and scudding along over the blue sparkling waves with equal celerity.

'Here I am, my dear friend,' said the Grand Prior to me as I handed him out of his brother the old Marquis of Marialva's most sleepifying dormeuse, which had been lent to him expressly for this *trying* occasion. 'Behold me at last,' (at last indeed, this being the third put-off I had experienced,) ever delighted with your company, but not so much so with the expedition we are going to undertake.'

'I hope it will not turn out so unpleasant after all,' was my answer: 'for my own part, I quite long to see Alcobaça.'

'So do not I,' rejoined the Grand Prior; 'but let that pass. Is Ehrhart come? is Franchi ready? Has the first secured the medicine-chest he was in such an agony about the other day, and the second the pianoforte he swore he would break to pieces unless it would get into better tune?'

'All safe – all waiting – and dinner too, my dear Lord Prior; and after that, let us get off. No easy matter, by the bye, even yet, some of the party being such adepts at dawdling.'

Why the Grand Prior should have dreaded the journey so much I really could not imagine, every pains having been taken to make it so easy and smooth. It was settled he should loll in his dormeuse or in my chaise just as he best pleased, and look at nothing calculated to excite the fatigue of reflection;

topographical inquiries were to be waived completely, and no questions asked about who endowed such a church or raised such a palace. We were to proceed, or rather creep along, by short and facile stages; stopping to dine, and sup, and repose, as delectably as in the most commodious of homes. Everything that could be thought of, or even dreamed of, for our convenience or relaxation, was to be carried in our train, and nothing left behind but Care and Sorrow; two spectres, who, had they dared to mount on our shoulders, would have been driven off with a high hand by the Prior of St. Vincent's, than whom a more delightful companion never existed since the days of those polished and gifted canons and cardinals who formed such a galaxy of talent and facetiousness round Leo the Tenth.

We were absolutely roused from our repast, over which the Prior of St. Vincent's gay animated conversation was throwing its usual brilliance, by a racket and hubbub on the sea-shore that was perfectly distracting. The space between my villa and the sea was entirely blocked up, half the population of Belem having poured forth to witness our departure. The lubberly drivers of the baggage-carts were fighting and squabbling amongst themselves for precedence. One of the most lumbering of these ill-constructed vehicles, laden with a large heavy marquee, had its hind wheels already well buffeted by the waves. At length it moved off; and then burst forth such vociferation and such deafening shouts of 'Long live the Prince!' and 'Long live the Marialvas, and all their friends into the bargain!' – the Englishman of course included – as I expected, would have fixed a headache for life upon the unhappy Grand Prior.

Amongst other noises which gave him no small annoyance, might be reckoned the outrageous snortings and neighings of both his favourite high-pampered chaise-horses, out of compliment to one of my delicate English mares, who was trying to get through the crowd with a most engaging air of sentimental retiring modesty.

Half laughing and half angry lest some unfortunate kick or plunge might deprive me of her agreeable services, I refrained not from crying out to the Grand Prior, 'For pity's sake, let us dawdle and doodle no longer, but drive through this mob if it be possible. You see what a disturbance the glorious fuss which

3

has been making about this journey has occasioned; you see the result of a surfeit of superfluities: really, if we had been setting forth to explore the kingdom of Prester John, or the identical spot where Don Sebastian left his bones, (if true it be that the shores of Africa, and not some pet dungeon of King Philip's, received them,) we could scarcely have gotten together a grander array of encumbrances. At this rate, we shall have occasion to put our tent in requisition this very night, unless we defer our journey again, and sleep under my roof at San José.'

'No, no,' said the Prior of St. Vincent's; 'we shall sleep at my convent's pleasant quinta of Tojal. I shall set off with my people immediately to prepare for your reception.'

The deed followed the word: his attendant muleteers cracked their whips in the most imposing style – his ferradors pushed on – the crowd divided – a passage was cleared; the Grand Prior, ordering his dormeuse to follow, got into my enormous travelling chaise, and by the efforts of six stout mules we soon reached Bemfica.

Beyond this village, a shady lane overhung by elms brought us to Nossa Senhora de Luz; a large pile of buildings in the majestic style which prevailed during the Spanish domination in Portugal, but much shattered by the earthquake. From hence we passed on to Lumiares, through intricate paved roads bordered by aloes, sprouting up to the height of ten or twelve feet, in shape and colour not unlike gigantic asparagus.

Lumiares contains a quinta belonging to the Marquess of Anjeja, upon which immense sums have been lavished for the wise purpose of pebbling alleys in quaint mosaic patterns, red, black, and blue; building colossal reservoirs for gold and silver fish, painting their smooth plastered sides with divers flaming colours, and cutting a steep hill into a succession of stiff terraces, under the sole pretext, one should think, of establishing flights of awkward narrow marble steps to communicate one with the other, for they did not appear to lead to any other part of the garden.

The road from Lumiares to Loures is conducted along a valley, between sloping acclivities variegated by fields of grain and wild shrubby pastures. The soft air of the evening was delightful; and the lowing of herds descending from the hills to slake their thirst after a sultry day, at springs and fountains, full of pastoral charm. It grew dark when we passed the village of Tojal, and crossing a bridge over the river Trancaõ, entered the woody domain of the monks of St. Vincent. Lights glimmering at the extremity of an avenue of orange-trees directed us to the house, a low picturesque building, half villa, half hermitage. Our reception was so truly exhilarating, so perfectly all in point of comfort and luxury that the heart of man or even churchman could desire, that we willingly promised to pass the whole of tomorrow in this cheerful residence, and defer our further progress till the day following.

SECOND DAY.

A Morning Walk.—Boundless Orchards of Orange and Apricot.—The River Trancaõ.—Magnificent Bay-tree.—A Fishing-party.—Happy Inclosure.—An Afternoon Ramble to the Palace of the Patriarch, and its immense Parterre.—Musical contest between Frogs and Nightingales.

4th June

The sunbeams entering my windows summoned me to enjoy the fresh morning breeze blowing over the uninterrupted mass of foliage which fills up the whole valley belonging to the convent.

After breakfast we walked amongst well-cultivated vegetables, fields of Indian wheat as healthy and vigorous as any that ever flourished in the islands which float about like rafts on the Lake of Mexico, and the most extensive orchards of orange, apricots, and other fruit trees, perhaps in Portugal. Every inch of ground within this enclosure is turned to the most advantageous account: the oranges alone produce from seven to eight thousand cruzados a year. A very active lay-brother has the management of this fortunate spot, and is continually extending its limits over the bare hills in the neighbourhood, many of which are comprised within the domain of the fathers.

The river Trancaõ, which runs through the garden, is diminished to a brook at this season; but that brook is clear, and flows rapidly. Its rocky edges, worn into irregular shapes by winter torrents, bloom with the rose-coloured flowers of the oleander. Their appearance was strikingly beautiful – many of these shrubs had attained the height of fifteen or sixteen feet.

But one of the grandest objects of the vegetable world which ever met my sight is a bay-tree, situated in the thickest part of the orange orchards, above which it towers majestically, clothed with luxuriant boughs that glisten with health and vigour. It consists of about thirty stems, none less than two feet, and some thirty-eight inches in diameter, springing from one root, and rising to the height of sixty-four feet. I loitered away the sultry hours of mid-day most pleasantly under its deep, fragrant shade.

The Prior had ordered a fishing-party for our amusement; – no great amusement, however, for one who detests the sight of wretched animals, inveigled from their cool aquatic homes, and cast on a dry bank, gasping for life and distending their jaws in torment. Full often have I fancied what woeful grimaces we children of Adam would be compelled to make, should ever the colossal inhabitants of a superior planet be permitted on some dread day of retribution to drop down on the earth on an angling tour, and fish us out of our element for their dinner or recreation. No want of sport need be apprehended in this case – plenty would bite. Men have in general such wide-open appetites for the objects of their individual pursuit, that, only render the bait sufficiently tempting, and I promise they swallow it, hook and all. So few set any bounds to their voraciousness, that a shark might be chosen president of a temperance society with equal justice. Courtesy obliged both the Grand Prior and Doctor Ehrhart, as well as myself, to remain much longer than we wished on the banks of the river, witnessing the joy of the anglers, and the struggles of the expiring fish.

About two, we returned home, through shady alleys of curious citron-trees, collected from every part of the Portuguese dominions on this and on the other side of the ocean, divided by tall canes mantled with vines, which promise, like every plant in this happy enclosure, an abundant produce. The nightingales were singing in the recesses of woods impenetrable to the sun, and at the same time, I am sorry to add, frogs were croaking a deep thorough-bass to this enchanting melody.

We dined late for the sake of devouring the produce of

our fishery, prepared by the fishermen themselves – a sort of matelotte, which my famous Simon, the most incomparable of cooks, declared, with a smile of ineffable contempt, was only fit to be placed before persons dying with hunger and cast away on some desolate island.

In the cool of the evening we drove through the village of Tojal to a palace of the Patriarch, containing nothing very remarkable, except a vestibule with a tribune looking into a church. The walls of this gallery are lined with the richest marbles of Spain and Portugal, disposed in panels, and ornamented with an overwhelming profusion of doubly and trebly gilt bronze ornaments, in that style of lavish expenditure carried to such triumphant excess by that most magnificent of modern Solomons, King John the Fifth.

After seeing ourselves reflected on all sides in tablets innumerable, polished like mirrors, we repaired to an immense parterre – the flattest, the richest in red and yellow flowers, and the most like a Turkey carpet, of any I ever had the vexation of visiting either in Holland or Germany. I was glad to escape from this far-spread expanse of pomposity and dullness, and return to the simple orange thickets of my amiable friend, where I walked till almost midnight, listening to the nightingales, who at length had shamed the frogs to silence.

THIRD DAY.

Curious Conversation with an Ex-missionary from China.— Wonders of the Imperial Gardens.—Strange Belief of the Emperor of China.

5th June

The first sounds I heard upon awakening this superiorly fine and glowing morning, was not 'the charm of early birds,' but the obstreperous rattle of a violent altercation, or, in simple truth, a downright squabble which broke out, in the vestibule adjoining my room, between the Grand Prior's secretary and a confidential attendant of my good friend of St. Vincent's.

'You know,' said the first-mentioned shrill-voiced consequential personage, 'my master is too lazy to stir from his shady quarters whilst the sun shines out in so fierce a manner,'

7

'You know,' answered the other, 'that we have business of urgency at Alcobaça, and the Prince Regent's command to perform it with the less delay the better.'

'You do not pretend,' rejoined the secretary, 'do you, to force on his Excellency whether he will or not?'

'What, does he mean to loiter the whole day in our garden of Eden? Shall we not advance as far as Cadafaiz in the cool of the evening?'

'Not we: his Excellency has made up his mind to take his fill of repose, and I am not the man to contradict him.'

'Then you are a rebellious fool for your pains, and have forgotten his royal highness's express orders. – Go on drinking the waters of Lethe if you dare.'

'Va beber,' &c. – 'Go, drink the filthiest puddle in these orchards,' rejoined the waspish and irritated secretary.

Tingle, tingle, tingle, went the Grand Prior's silver bell; off ran the disputants, and out came I into the vast echoing vestibule, opening, by as many glazed doors as there are days in a month, into the orange orchards.

If ever a decent excuse could be offered for perfect laziness, it was to be found in the warm, enervating atmosphere, loaded with perfume, which universally invested this pleasant umbrageous region. No wonder my Lord of Aviz, the most consummate professor of 'il dolce far niente' in all Portugal, and Algarve to boot, could not be withdrawn from it without infinite reluctance. He could hardly even be persuaded to traverse a short avenue which led to a summer pavilion on the banks of the river, where our morning collation was prepared. The Prior of St. Vincent's had a sort of romantic scheme of having our repast spread out on a little remnant of green-sward which the heats had spared, and sitting down to it in the Oriental style; but his illustrious colleague gently intimated a preference to chairs and tables.

In addition to our usual party I found a certain padre, Machado, or Azevedo, or some such name, who had not been long returned from China – nay, from Pekin itself. During his residence at Macao, he had learnt sufficient English from one of the padres of our Canton factory – the chaplain, I suppose – to read Sir William Chambers' most florid essay on Chinese gardening. I asked him how many words of truth there might happen to be in all this luxuriant description? He answered, not in plain English, but in a most delectable jargon, half Chinese sing-song, half lingua franca – 'There be ten-tousand-time-ten-tousand.'

'You don't mean to assure me,' said I, 'that our famous architect's most wonderful account of the magical splendour of Yven-ming-Yven and Tchang-tchung-Yven is not exaggerated?'

'It is not,' answered the padre in sound Portuguese, having quitted the straits and shallows of very scanty English for the full flow of his vernacular language: – 'I have seen greater wonders than he – I have seen in the depth of winter a whole extent of garden warmed by a deliciously mild and scented vapour, and all the trees covered with silken leaves and artificial flowers, and, on a pool of water, as clear and transparent as the sky it reflected, hundreds of gaily-enamelled ducks, formed of metal, swimming by mechanism, and by mechanism opening all their bills and uttering their accustomed sound with their usual volubility, and swallowing the food the eunuchs of the palace cast to them, – ay, and returning it again, to all appearance most happily digested, the emperor standing by all the while, laughing at my surprise, and believing himself neither more nor less, I am entirely convinced, than an incarnation of the god Fo!'

'Dreadful!' exclaimed the Grand Prior: 'I wonder he has not shared the fate of Nebuchadnezzar!'

'He should have been sent to grass at once,' observed the Prior of St. Vincent's.

'That would have been a pity,' rejoined the ex-missionary; 'for, notwithstanding his Tartarian nonsense about incarnations and such like, and the impossibility I experienced of making him comprehend our own ineffable mysteries, I must declare him to be a wise monarch and an excellent man.'

'That is more difficult to believe than all you have told us,' observed the Grand Prior, 'when we reflect upon the horrid impiety of believing one's self Fo.'

'There is no lie in the world people will not believe,' replied the missionary, 'provided they are often told it by flatterers in whom, for the very reason they ought not, they take delight in placing confidence; and when all the princes of the blood, all the courtiers, and all the mandarins of the different tribunals, are continually pouring forth addresses at the foot of the throne, assuring his imperial majesty Kien-Long, that he is the son of heaven, a god upon earth! what would you have him do?'

'Go to the devil his own way, as there is no other remedy,' said our hospitable host with a hearty laugh. 'We are to conclude, no doubt, you did your best to bring him round: perhaps you may succeed better another time.' – (The padre was on the eve of returning to his mission.) – 'And now let us go to mass,' continued the Prior, bowing to his Excellency of Aviz, 'and pray for the emperor's conversion!'

So to mass they went, and then a-fishing; and the evening of this day was like the morning all warmth, and chat, and idleness.

FOURTH DAY
A first-rate Blessing.—The Duke d'Alafoens' Chateau.—The great Highway to the Caldas.—Extensive Fertility.—Cadafaiz.— Boundless Vineyard.—Eggs of the Sun.—A calm Retirement.— Peaceful State of Portugal compared to other parts of the Continent.

6th June

At length it pleased heaven to inspire the Grand Prior with sufficient resolution to proceed; the last dregs of excuses for loitering being exhausted. The air had become much cooler; and the sun being overcast, we experienced a first-rate blessing – that of travelling under a canopy of clouds, which had the kindness not to disperse till we passed Al Priate, a chateau belonging to the Duke d'Alafoens.

This sumptuous abode, with pompous high roofs, and courts, and avenues, as Frenchified as their illustrious master, is placed in a valley which would have been pleasant enough had any other trees except the pale leaden-coloured olive happened to predominate.

After jolting along in rather a convulsive manner for about a league, and receiving many a pinch from my alarmed and nervous companion, we emerged from a chaos of ruts and sandbanks into the great highway which leads to the Caldas through Alhandra, Povos, and Villa Franca.

All these places, not unpleasantly situated on the banks of the Tagus, have quintas, palaces, and fidalgos, as well as their betters; but the country which surrounds them is pretty nearly as flat, and as rich in ditches, sluices, and other means of irrigation, as the environs of Antwerp itself. Her most faithful majesty sometimes resorting to the Caldas, the road is kept in tolerable repair.

At every league, pedestals with vases upon them meet the eye; and at no very distant intervals, architectural fountains, which have not yet entirely forgotten the purpose for which they were erected, and still contrive to dribble out a scanty and turbid stream.

As we approached Carregado, scenes of boundless plenty began to expand themselves; unlimited fields of Turkish corn, fine barley, and black Sicilian wheat, the ears bending to the ground with their weight.

We now abandoned the high road in order to reach Cadafaiz, another ample domain under the government of our hospitable friend, where we arrived late in the afternoon. There we found ourselves in a most comfortable antiquated mansion, perfectly cool and clean; the floors neatly matted, the tables covered with the finest white linen, and, in bright clear caraffes of Venetian glass, the most beautiful carnations I ever met with, even at Genoa in the Durazzo Gardens.

The wide latticed windows of the apartment allotted to me commanded the view of a boundless vineyard in full luxuriant leaf, divided by long broad tracts of thyme and camomile, admirably well kept and nicely weeded. From this immense sea of green leaves rose a number of plum, pear, orange, and apricot trees; the latter procured by the monks directly from Damascus, and bearing, as I can testify, that most delicious fruit of its kind called 'eggs of the sun' by the Persians; – even insects and worms seem to respect it, for no trace could I discover of their having preyed on its smooth glowing rind and surrounding foliage.

Beyond these truly Hesperian orchards, very lofty hills swell into the most picturesque forms, varied by ledges of rock, and completely enclose this calm retirement; wild healthful spots of delicate herbage, which the goats and sheep, whose bells I heard tinkling in the distance, are scarcely more partial to than myself.

How often, contrasting my present situation with the horrid disturbed state of almost every part of the Continent, did I bless the hour when my steps were directed to Portugal! As I sat in the nook of my retired window, I looked with complacency on a roof which sheltered no scheming hypocrites, – on tables, on which perhaps no newspaper had ever been thrown, and on neat white pillows, guiltless of propping up the heads of those assassins of real prosperity – political adventurers. The very air which kept playing around my temples seemed to breathe contentment; it was genially warm, not oppressive, and brought with it the intermingled fragrance of mountain herbs and native flowers.

FIFTH DAY

A Ramble over the Hills.—Beautiful Grotto.—Reminiscences of Gil Blas.—Journey resumed.—First Sight of Alcobaça.—Pompous Reception.—The Three Graces of Holiness.—Gloomy Church.—Sepulchral Chapel of Pedro the Just and Inez.—Interrupted Reveries.—Enormous Kitchen.—Hospitable Preparations.—The Banquet Hall.—The Banquet.—Tiresome Minuets.—Ineffectual Offer.—Ceremonious 'Good Nights.'

7th June

Not long after daybreak, whilst all the dews of the morning were still waiting to be dried up, I took a ramble over the hills, and, on one of their level summits, discovered an irregular opening with rude steps leading down to a little cavern hewn out of a pumice rock, blessed with a tinkling spring, and mantled all over with the deliciously-scented flowers of the Lonicera tribe in wild luxuriant profusion, – exactly the sort of grotto described in Gil Blas as the resort of Algerine pirates. There I proposed reading my favourite pocket-companions Monteiro and Manoel Maria Bocage, in total solitude, and sharing the deep reveries of these intellectual and Cowley-like poets: but fate denied me the enjoyment of such dreamy happiness. The sober reality of proceeding on our expedition, and particularly of paying a visit to the Caldas, was enforced by my right reverend conductors.

Having a presentiment that the said Caldas were as hot as the suburbs at least of the infernal regions, I begged and entreated we might not stop at such a close, stifling, unpoetical place, but, after taking refreshment under our tent in the open country, make the best of our way boldly and resolutely to Alcobaça. 'Impossible!' said the Grand Prior. 'Possible!' exclaimed the Prior of St. Vincent. The vote of the latter carried it, and we got on three or four leagues at a good round pace; the bells of our mules sounding cheerily, and their drivers singing in chorus, to the surprise, if not delight, of my English grooms and attendants.

Thus far all had gone on, as to road, pretty tolerably; but we had scarcely left the Caldas in arrear about two miles on the right, before 'the way was all before us where to choose;' no distinct track for such lumbering carriages as we were burthened with being visible. In attempting to advance, we stuck fast: both the mules and their drivers seemed so sincerely alarmed at the prospect before them, and reduced to such utter despair, that my right reverend fellow-travellers, who most fully sympathised in these not unfounded terrors, determined to call the posse comitatus to our aid. A messenger was despatched for that purpose to a neighbouring village, of which I never suspected the existence, it being completely buried in a deep narrow ravine, not unlike one of those enormous ruts which many people fancy they have discovered in the moon. The messenger soon returned with a very efficient magistrate, and thirty or forty stout well-clothed peasants.

A village Hercules putting his shoulder to the wheel, we got out of this scrape; but it was only to fall into another, and so on from bad to worse till patience itself was exhausted. The day was wearing apace; we had not advanced upon our voyage of discovery at the rate of above three miles in two hours. The carriages laboured and rolled like vessels on a swelling sea after a storm. At length ropes were applied to steady them, deafening shouts of encouragement addressed to men and mules, and in an hour more we were approaching Alcobaça.

The first sight of this regal monastery is very imposing; and the picturesque, well-wooded and well-watered village, out of the quiet bosom of which it appears to rise, relieves the mind from a sense of oppression the huge domineering bulk of the conventual buildings inspire.

We had no sooner hove in sight, and we loomed large, than a most tremendous ring of bells of extraordinary power announced our speedy arrival. A special aviso, or broad hint from the secretary of state, recommending these magnificent monks to receive the Grand Prior and his companions with peculiar graciousness, the whole community, including fathers, friars, and subordinates, at least four hundred strong, were drawn up in grand spiritual array on the vast platform before the monastery to bid us welcome. At their head the Abbot himself, in his costume of High Almoner of Portugal, advanced to give us a cordial embrace.

It was quite delectable to witness with what cooings and comfortings the Lord Abbot of Alcobaça greeted his right reverend brethren of Aviz and St. Vincent's – turtle-doves were never more fondlesome, at least in outward appearance. Preceded by these three graces of holiness, I entered the spacious, massive, and somewhat austere Saxon-looking church. All was gloom, except where the perpetual lamps burning before the high altar diffused a light most solemn and religious – (inferior twinkles from side chapels and chantries are not worth mentioning). To this altar my high clerical conductors repaired, whilst the full harmonious tones of several stately organs, accompanied by the choir, proclaimed that they were in the act of adoring the real Presence.

Whilst these devout prostrations were performing, I lost not a moment in visiting the sepulchral chapel, where lie interred Pedro the Just and his beloved Inez. The light which reached this solemn recess of a most solemn edifice was so subdued and hazy, that I could hardly distinguish the elaborate sculpture of the tomb, which reminded me, both as to design and execution, of the Beauchamp monument at Warwick, so rich in fretwork and imagery.

Just as I was giving way to the affecting reveries which such an object could not fail of exciting in a bosom the least susceptible of romantic impressions, in came the Grand Priors hand in hand, all three together. 'To the kitchen,' said they in perfect unison, – 'to the kitchen, and that immediately; you will then judge whether we have been wanting in zeal to regale you.'

Such a summons, so conveyed, was irresistible; the three prelates led the way to, I verily believe, the most distinguished temple of gluttony in all Europe. What Glastonbury may have been in its palmy state, I cannot answer; but my eyes never beheld in any modern convent of France, Italy, or Germany, such an enormous space dedicated to culinary purposes. Through the centre of the immense and nobly-groined hall, not less than sixty feet in diameter, ran a brisk rivulet of the clearest water, flowing through pierced wooden reservoirs, containing every sort and size of the finest river-fish. On one side, loads of game and venison were heaped up; on the other, vegetables and fruit in endless variety. Beyond a long line of stoves extended a row of ovens, and close to them hillocks of wheaten flour whiter than snow, rocks of sugar, jars of the purest oil, and pastry in vast abundance, which a numerous tribe of lay brothers and their attendants were rolling out and puffing up into an hundred different shapes, singing all the while as blithely as larks in a corn-field.

My servants, and those of their reverend excellencies the two Priors, were standing by in the full glee of witnessing these hospitable preparations, as well pleased, and as much flushed, as if they had been just returned from assisting at the marriage at Cana in Galilee. 'There,' said the Lord Abbot, – 'we shall not starve: God's bounties are great, it is fit we should enjoy them.' – (By the bye, I thought this allegro, contrasted with the penseroso of scarecrow convents, quite delightful.) – 'An hour hence supper will be ready,' continued the Lord Abbot, 'in the meanwhile, let me conduct you to your apartment; it has only bare walls, for we learnt of your arrival too late this morning to put up our fine hangings.'

I found the apartment, which was composed of an ante-room, saloon, and bedchamber, lofty and rather pleasant. Though the walls were naked, the ceiling was gilt and painted, the floor spread with Persian carpets of the finest texture, and the tables in rich velvet petticoats, decked out with superb ewers and basins of chased silver, and towels bordered with point-lace of a curious antique pattern, – a strange mixture of simplicity and magnificence. I had my own bed pitched in one of the spacious alcoves, to the apparent surprise, if not displeasure, of the monk appointed to give me attendance. However, I made myself very comfortable; took a foot-bath as serenely as if I had been at Abraham's tent-door, and waited in a perfect refreshing calm till three thundering knocks at the outward portal announced the Abbot himself coming to lead me to the banquet-hall.

We passed through a succession of cloisters and galleries, which the shades of evening rendered dimly visible, till we entered a saloon, superb, indeed, covered with pictures, and lighted up by a profusion of wax tapers in sconces of silver. Right in the centre of this stately room stood a most ample table, covered with fringed embroidered linen, and round it four ponderous fauteuils for the guest and the three prelates; so we formed a very comfortable *partie quarrée.*

The banquet itself consisted of not only the most excellent usual fare, but rarities and delicacies of past seasons and distant countries; exquisite sausages, potted lampreys, strange messes from the Brazils, and others still stranger from China (edible birds' nests and sharks' fins), dressed after the latest mode of Macao by a Chinese lay brother. Confectionery and fruits were out of the question here; they awaited us in an adjoining still more spacious and sumptuous apartment, to which we retired from the effluvia of viands and sauces.

In this apartment we found Franchi and the Grand Prior of Aviz's secretary, the Prior of St. Vincent's acolyte, and ten or twelve principal personages of the neighbourhood, most eager to enjoy a stare at the stranger whom their lordly abbot delighted to honour. The table being removed, four good-looking novices, lads of fifteen or sixteen, demure even to primness, came in, bearing cassolettes of Goa filigree, steaming with a fragrant vapour of Calambac, the finest quality of wood of aloes.

This pleasing ceremony performed, the saloon was cleared out as if for dancing. I flattered myself we were going to be favoured with a bolero, fandango, or perhaps the fofa itself, – a dance as decent as the ballets exhibited for the recreation of Muley Liezit, his most exemplary Marocchese majesty. A crowd of clarionet and guitar players, dressed in silk dominoes like the serenaders in Italian burlettas, followed by a posse of young monks and young gentlemen in secular dresses as stiff as buckram, began an endless succession of the most decorous and tiresome minuets I ever witnessed, ten times longer, and alas! ten times less ridiculous, than even the long minuet at Bath.

Tired to death of remaining motionless, and desirous of exhibiting something a little out of the common way, I gently hinted a wish to dance, and that I should have no objection were one of the three right reverend Priors to take me out. It would not do – they kept their state. Yawning piteously, I longed for the hour when it should become lawful to retire to bed; which I did right gladly when the blessed hour came, after good-nighting, and being good-nighted with another round of ceremony.

SIXTH DAY

Endless Corridors and a grim-looking Hall.—Portrait of St. Thomas à Becket.—Ancient Cloister.—Venerable Orange-trees.— Sepulchral Inscriptions.—The Refectory.—Solemn Summons to Breakfast.—Sights.—Gorgeous Sacristy.—Antiquities.— Precious Specimen of Early Art.—Hour of Siesta.—A Noon-day Ramble.—Silence and Solitude.—Mysterious Lane.—Irresistible Somnolency of my Conductor.—An unseen Songstress.—A Surprise.—Donna Francisca, her Mother and Confessor.—The World of Alcobaça awakened.—Return to the Monastery.— Departure for Batalha.—The Field of Aljubarota.—Solitary Vale.—Reception at Batalha.—Enormous Supper.—Ecstasies of an old Monk.—His sentimental Mishap.—Night Scene.—Awful Denunciations.

8th June

I rose early, slipped out of my pompous apartment, strayed about endless corridors – not a soul stirring. Looked into a gloomy hall, much encumbered with gilded ornaments, and grim with the ill-sculptured effigies of kings; and another immense chamber, with white walls covered with pictures in black lacquered frames, most hideously unharmonious.

One portrait, the full size of life, by a very ancient Portuguese artist named Vasquez, attracted my minute attention. It repre-sented no less interesting a personage than St. Thomas à Becket, and looked the character in perfection; – lofty in stature and expression of countenance; pale, but resolute, like one devoted to death in his great cause; the very being Dr. Lingard has portrayed in his admirable History.

From this chamber I wandered down several flights of stairs to a cloister of the earliest Norman architecture, having in the centre a fountain of very primitive form, spouting forth clear water abundantly into a marble basin. Twisting and straggling over this uncouth mass of sculpture are several orange-trees, gnarled and crabbed, but covered with fruit and flowers, their branches grotesque and fantastic, exactly such as a Japanese would delight in, and copy on his caskets and screens; their age most venerable, for the traditions of the convent assured me that they were the very first imported from China into Portugal. There was some comfort in these objects; every other in the place looked dingy and dismal, and steeped in a green and yellow melancholy.

On the damp, stained and mossy walls, I noticed vast numbers of sepulchral inscriptions (some nearly effaced) to the memory of the knights slain at the battle of Aljubarota: I gave myself no trouble to make them out, but continuing my solitary ramble, visited the refectory, a square of seventy or eighty feet, be-gloomed by dark-coloured painted windows, and disgraced by tables covered with not the cleanest or least unctuous linen in the world.

I had proceeded thus far, when three venerable fathers, of most grave and solemn aspect, made their appearance; to whom having bowed as lowly as Abraham did to his angelic visitors, I received as many profound obeisances in return, and a summons to breakfast. This I readily obeyed: it wanted three-quarters of eight, and I was as hungry as a stripling novice. The Prior of Aviz having supped too amply the night before, did not appear; but he of St. Vincent's, all kindness and good digestion, did the honours with cordial grace, and made tea as skilfully as the most complete old dowager in Christendom. My Lord of Alcobaça was absent, – engaged, as I was told, and readily believed, upon conventual affairs of urgent importance.

The repast finished, and not soon, our whole morning was taken up with seeing sights, though not exactly the sights I most wished to see. Some MSS. of the fourteenth century, containing, I have been assured, traditional records of Pedro the Just and the Severe, were what I wished for; but they either could not or would not be found; and instead of being allowed to make this interesting research, or having it made for me, we were conducted to a most gorgeous and glistening sacristy, worthy of Versailles itself, adorned with furbelows of gilt bronze, flaunting over panels of jasper and porphyry: copes and vestments, some almost as ancient as the reign of Alfonzo Henriquez, and others embroidered at Rome with gold and pearl, by no means barbaric, were displayed before us in endless succession.

One of the sacristans or treasurers who happened to have a spice of antiquarianism, guessing the bent of my wishes, produced, from a press or ambery elaborately carved, the identical candlesticks of rock-crystal, and a cross of the same material, studded with the most delicately-tinted sapphires; which were taken by the victorious John the First from the King of Castile's portable chapel, after the hard-fought conflict of Aljubarota; and several golden reliquaries, as minutely chased and sculptured as any I ever saw at St. Denis, though wrought by St. Eloy's holy hands: one in particular, the model of a cathedral in the style of the Sainte Chapelle at Paris, struck me as being admirable. Ten times at least did I examine and almost worship this highly-wrought precious specimen of early art, and as many times did my excellent friend the Prior of St. Vincent's, who had come in search of me, express a wish that I should not absolutely wear out my eyes or his patience.

'It is growing insufferably warm,' said he, 'and the hour of siesta is arrived; and I cannot help thinking that perhaps it would not be unpleasant for you to retire to your shady chamber: for my part, I can hardly keep my eyes open any longer. But I see this proposal does not suit you – you English are strangely given to locomotion, and I know full well that of all English you are not the least nimble. Here,' continued he, calling a young monk, who was sitting by in a nook of the sacristy peeling walnuts, 'suspend that important occupation, and be pleased to accompany this fidalgo to any part of your domain he likes to ramble to.'

'Right willingly,' answered this sprout of holiness: 'whither shall we go?'

'Through the village, into the open country, if you have no objection,' answered I; 'to any point, in short, where I may enjoy rural scenery, trees, and rocks, and running waters.'

'Trees, and rocks, and running waters!' re-echoed the monk with a vacant stare. 'Had you not better visit our rabbit-warren – the finest in this world? Though, to be sure, the rabbits, poor things! are all asleep at this time of day, and it would be cruel to disturb even them.'

This was a broad hint, but I would not take it. The monk, finding I was bent on he could not imagine what pursuit, and that there was no diverting me from it, tucked up his upper garments, shadowed his sleek round face with an enormous straw hat, offered me another of equal size quite new and glossy, and, with staves in our hands, we set forth like the disciples journeying to Emmaus in some of Poelemburg's smooth landscapes.

We passed through quadrangles after quadrangles, and courts after courts, till, opening a sly door in an obscure corner, which had proved a convenient sally-port, no doubt, for many an agreeable excursion, we found ourselves in a winding alley, bordered by sheds and cottages, with irregular steps leading up to rustic porches and many a vine-bower and many a trellised walk. No human being was to be heard or seen; no poultry were parading about; and except a beautiful white macaw perched on a broken wall, and nestling his bill under his feathers, not a single member of the feathered creation was visible. There was a holy calm in this mid-day silence – a sacredness, as if all nature had been fearful to disturb the slumbers of universal Pan.

I kept, however, straggling on – impiously, it would have been thought in Pagan times – between long stretches of garden-walls overhung by fig-trees, the air so profoundly tranquil that I actually heard a fruit drop from a bough. Sometimes I was enticed down a mysterious lane by the prospect of a crag and a Moorish castle which offered itself to view at its termination, and sometimes under ruined arches which crossed my path in the most picturesque manner. So I still continued my devious course with a pertinacity that annoyed my lazy conductor – past utterance, it seems; for during our whole excursion we scarcely exchanged a syllable.

At length, he could bear with my romanceishness no longer; an irresistible somnolency came over him; and, stretching himself out on the bare ground, in the deep shadow of some tall cypress, he gave way to repose most delectably. I was now abandoned entirely to myself, unsubdued by the quiet of the place, and as active as ever. Some tokens of animation, however, in other beings besides myself would not have been displeasing – the dead silence which prevailed began to oppress me.

At length, a faint musical murmur stole upon my ear: I advanced towards the spot whence it seemed to come – a retired garden-house at the end of a pleasant avenue, which, to add to its pleasantness, had been lately watered. Drawing nearer and nearer, my heart beating quickly all the while, I distinguished the thrilling cadences of a delightful Brasileira (*sinha the vem da Bahia*), – well-known sounds. I looked up to a latticed window just thrown open by a lovely arm – a well-known arm: – 'Gracious heavens! Donna Francisca, is it you? What brought you here? What inspired you to exchange Queluz and the Ajuda for this obscure retirement?'

'Ascend these steps, and I will tell you: but your stay must not exceed ten minutes – not a second more.'

'Brief indeed,' answered I: 'I see there is no time to lose.'

Up I sprung – and who should receive me? Not the fascinating songstress – not the lady of the lovely arm, but her sedate though very indulgent mother.

'I know whom you are looking for,' said the matron; 'but it is in vain. You have heard, but are not to see, Francisca, who is no longer the giddy girl you used to dance with; her heart is turned, – nay, do not look so wild, – turned, I tell you, but turned to God. A most holy man, a saint, the very mirror of piety for his years – he is not yet forty, only think! – operated this blessed change. You know how light-hearted, and almost indiscreetly so, my poor dear heart's comfort was. You recollect hearing, and you were terribly angry, I remember, that the English Padre told the Inviada it was shameful how very rapturously my poor dear girl rattled her castanets, and threw back her head, and put forward every other part of her dear little person, at the Factory ball – Shame ON HIM, scandalous old crabbed heretic! Well, it so happened that my Lord High Almoner came to court upon state affairs, accompanied by the precious man I have been talking of, – the most exemplary monk in that noble convent, and its right hand. One day at Queluz he saw my daughter dancing divinely, as you know she did; he heard her sing, – you know how she warbles – she still warbles; HE said, (and he has such an eye,) that under the veil of all this levity were lurking the seeds of grace. 'I will develop them,' exclaimed this saint upon earth, in a transport of holy fervour. So he set about it, – and a miraculous metamorphosis did he perform: my gay, my dissipated child, became an example of serious piety; no flirting, no racketing, nothing but pious discourse with this best of discoursers. Two months passed away in this exemplary manner. When the time came for my Lord High Almoner to return, our holy friend was in duty bound to accompany him. What was to be done? Francisca had forgotten everything and everybody else in this sinful world; she existed but for this devout personage; she lived but in his holy smiles when he approved her conduct, and almost died under his reproof when any transient little fault of hers occasioned his enjoining her severe penances: and I shudder to think how severe they sometimes were; for, would you believe it? he has made her submit to flagellation – and, more than once, to goadings with sharp points. In due course, the hour of departure arrived. 'We must all die,' said Francisca; 'my hour is come.' She looked all she said she pined and languished, and, I am convinced, would have kept her word, if I had not said, 'Dearest child, there is but one remedy: it is the will of God we should go to Alcobaça; and to Alcobaça we will go, let all your uncles, cousins, and adorers say what they choose to the contrary.' So we took this house and this garden – a nice little garden – only look at these pretty yellow carnations! – and we are very happy in our little way, entirely given up to devotion, under the guidance of our incomparable spiritual director, who allows us to want for nothing, even in this world. See what fruit! what fine sweetmeats! what a relishing Melgaço ham! look at these baskets!'

She was just lifting up the rich damask covers thrown over them, when a most vigorous 'Hem! hem!! hem!!!' in the rustic street snapped short the thread of her eloquence, by calling her to the balcony with the utmost precipitation – 'Jesu Maria José! – he comes! he comes!' Had she seen a ghost instead of a very substantial friar, she could not have started with greater abruptness: her scared looks showed me the door so intelligibly that I was off in a twinkling; it would have been most indiscreet – nay, sacrilegious, to remain a moment longer.

It was now half-past one, and the world of Alcobaça was alive again – the peasant had resumed her distaff, the monk his breviary, the ox his labour, and the sound of the nora, or water-wheel, was heard in the land. The important hour of dinner at the convent I knew was approaching: I wished to scale the crag above the village, and visit the Moorish castle, which looked most invitingly picturesque, with its varied outline of wall and tower; but I saw a possé of monks and novices advancing from the convent, bowing and beckoning me to return.

So I returned, – and 'twas well I did, as it turned out. Fourteen or fifteen sleek well-fed mules, laden with paniers of neat wicker-work, partially covered with scarlet cloth, were standing about the grand platform before the convent; and the reverend father, one of the prime dignitaries of the chapter, who was waiting at the entrance of the apartment assigned to me, pointing to them, put me in mind that last night I had expressed a vehement wish to visit Batalha; adding most graciously, that the wishes of a person so strongly recommended to them as I had been by the good and great Marquis of Ponte de Lima were laws.

'This very, night, if it so please you,' said his reverence, 'we sleep at Batalha. The convent is poor and destitute, unworthy – nay, incapable of accommodating such guests as my lords the Grand Priors, and yourself; but I hope we have provided against the chill of a meagre reception. These mules will carry with them whatever may be required for your comfort. Tomorrow, I hope, you will return to us; and the following day, should you inflict upon us the misfortune of losing your delightful society, myself and two of my comrades will have the honour of accompanying you as far back as one of our farms called Pedraneira, on your return to Lisbon.'

There was nothing on my part to object to in this arrangement; I fancied too I could discern in it a lurking wish to be quit of our most delightful society, and the turmoil and half-partial restraint it occasioned. Putting on the sweetest smiles of grate-ful acquiescence, to hear was to obey; everything relating to movements being confirmed by the terzetto of Grand Priors during our repast – copious and splendid as usual.

The carriages drew up very soon after it was ended; my riding horses were brought out, all our respective attendants mustered, and, preceded by a long string of sumpter-mules and baggage-carts, with all their bells in full jingle and all their drivers in full cry; off we set in most formidable array, taking the route of Aljubarota.

Our road, not half so rough as I expected, led us up most picturesquely-shaped steep acclivities, shaded by chesnuts, with here and there a branching pine, for about a league. We then found ourselves on a sort of table-land; and, a mile or two further, in the midst of a straggling village. There was no temptation to leave the snug corner of our comfortable chaises; so we contented ourselves with surveying at our perfect ease the prospect of the famous plain, which formed the termination of a long perspective of antiquated houses.

Here, on this very plain, was fought in 1385 the fierce battle which placed the diadem of Portugal on the brow of the glorious and intrepid bastard. It was down that ravine the Castilian cavalry poured along in utter confusion, so hotly pursued that three thousand were slain. On yonder mound stood the King of Castile's tent and temporary chapel, which he abandoned, with all its rich and jewelled furniture, to the conquerors, and scampered off in such alarm that he scarcely knew whether he had preserved his head on his shoulders, till safe within the walls of Santarem, where he tore his hair and plucked off his beard by handfuls, and raved and ranted like a maniac. – The details of this frantic pluckage are to be found in a letter from the Constable Nuno Alvarez Pereira to the Abbot of Alcobaça.

I tried to inspire my right reverend fellow-travellers with patriotic enthusiasm, and to engage them to cast a retrospective glance upon the days of Lusitanian glory. Times present, and a few flasks of most exquisite wine, the produce of a neighbouring vineyard, engrossed their whole attention. 'Muito bom – primoroso – excellente,' were the only words that escaped their most grateful lips.

The Juiz de Fora of the village, a dabbler in history – for he told us he had read the Chronicles, and who stood courteously and obsequiously on the step of our carriage-door, handing us the precious beverage – made some attempts to edge in a word about the battle, and particularly about a certain valiant English knight, whose name he did not even pretend to remember, but who might have been a relation of mine for aught he knew to the contrary.

Well, this valiant knight, who had vanquished all the chivalry of France and England, had the honour of being vanquished in his turn by the flower of warriors, the renowned Magrico: a great honour too, for Magrivo had excellent taste in the choice of his antagonists, and would only fight with the bravest of the brave. 'Even so,' continued the worthy magistrate, bowing to the earth, 'as our great Camoëns testifies.' – No answer to all this flourish except 'Ten thousand thanks for your excellent wine: drive on.' And drive on we did with redoubled briskness.

The highest exhilaration prevailed throughout our whole caravan. All my English servants were in raptures, ready to turn Catholics. My famous French cook, in the glow of the moment, unpatriotically declared Clos de Vougeot, puddle compared to Aljubarota, – divine, perfumed, ethereal Aljubarota! Dr. Ehrhart protested no country under the sun equalled Portugal for curiosities in mineralogy, theology, and wineology – which ology he was now convinced was the best of them all. Franchi mounted one of my swiftest coursers – he had never ventured to mount before – and galloped away like the King of Castile on his flight to Santarem. The Grand Prior and all his ecclesiastical cortege fell fast asleep; and it would have been most irreverent not to have followed so respectable an example. I can therefore describe nothing of the remainder of our route.

The sun had sunk and the moon risen, when a tremendous jolt and a loud scream awakened the whole party. Poor Franchi lay sprawling upon the ground; whilst my Arabian, his glossy sides streaming with blood, was darting along like one of the steeds in the Apocalypse; happily his cast-off rider escaped with a slight contusion.

My eyes being fairly open, I beheld a quiet solitary vale, bordered by shrubby hills; a few huts, and but a few, peeping out of dense masses of foliage; and high above their almost level surface, the great church, with its rich cluster of abbatial buildings, buttresses, and pinnacles, and fretted spires, towering in all their pride, and marking the ground with deep shadows that appeared interminable, so far and so wide were they stretched along. Lights glimmered here and there in various parts of the edifice; but a strong glare of torches pointed out its principal entrance, where stood the whole community waiting to receive us.

Whilst our sumpter-mules were unlading, and ham and pies and sausages were rolling out of plethoric hampers, I thought these poor monks looked on rather enviously. My more fortunate companions – no wretched cadets of the mortification family, but the true elder sons of fat mother church – could hardly conceal their sneers of conscious superiority. A contrast so strongly marked amused me not a little.

The space before the entrance being narrow, there was some difficulty in threading our way through a labyrinth of panniers, and coffers, and baggage, – and mules, as obstinate as their drunken drivers, which is saying a great deal, – and all our grooms, lackeys, and attendants, half asleep, half muddled.

The Batalha Prior and his assistants looked quite astounded when they saw a gauze-curtained bed, and the Grand Prior's fringed pillow, and the Prior of St. Vincent's superb coverlid, and basins, and ewers, and other utensils of glittering silver, being carried in. Poor souls! they hardly knew what to do, to say, or be at one running to the right, another to the left – one tucking up his flowing garments to run faster, and another rebuking him for such a deviation from monastic decorum.

At length, order being somewhat re-established, and some fine painted wax tapers, which were just unpacked, lighted, we were ushered into a large plain chamber, and the heads of the order presented by the humble Prior of Batalha to their superior mightinesses of San Vicente and Aviz. Then followed a good deal of gossiping chat, endless compliments, still longer litanies, and an enormous supper.

One of the monks who partook of it, though almost bent double with age, played his part in excellent style. Animated by ample potations of the very best Aljubarota that ever grew, and which we had taken the provident care to bring with us, he exclaimed lustily, 'Well, this is as it should be – rare doings! such as have not been witnessed at Batalha since a certain progress that great King, John the Fifth, made hither more than half a century ago. I remember every circumstance attending it as clearly as though it had only taken place last week. But only think of the atrocious impudence of the gout! His blessed Majesty had hardly set down to a banquet ten times finer than this, before that accursed malady, patronized by all the devils in hell, thrust its fangs into his toe. I was at that period in the commencement of my noviciate, a handsome lad enough, and had the much-envied honour of laying a cloth of gold cushion under the august feet of our glorious sovereign. No sooner had the extremities of his royal person come in contact with the stiff embroidery, than he roared out as a mere mortal would have done, and looked as black as a thunder-storm; but soon recovering his most happy benign temper, gave me a rouleau of fine, bright, golden coin, and a tap on the head, – ay, on this once comely, now poor old shrivelled head. Oh, he was a gracious, open-hearted, glorious monarch – the very King of Diamonds and Lord of Hearts! Oh, he is in Heaven, in Heaven above! as sure – ay, as sure as I drink your health, most esteemed stranger.'

So saying, he drained a huge silver goblet to the last drop, and falling back in his chair, was carried out, chair and all, weeping, puling, and worse than drivelling, with such maudlin tenderness that he actually marked his track with a flow of liquid sorrows.

As soon as an act of oblivion had been passed over this little sentimental mishap by effacing every trace of it, we all rose up and retired to rest: but little rest, however, was in store for me; the heat of my mid-day ramble, and perhaps some baneful effect from our moon-lit journey, the rays of our cold satellite having fallen whilst I was asleep too directly on my head, had disordered me; I felt disturbed and feverish, a strange jumble of ideas and recollections fermented in my brain – springing in part. from the indignant feelings which Donna Francisca's fervour for her monk, and coldness for me, had inspired. I had no wish to sleep, and yet my pleasant retired chamber, with clean white walls, chequered with the reflection of waving boughs, and the sound of a rivulet softened by distance, invited it soothingly. Seating myself in the deep recess of a capacious window which was wide open, I suffered the balsamic air and serene moonlight to quiet my agitated spirits. One lonely nightingale had taken possession of a bay-tree just beneath me, and was pouring forth its ecstatic notes at distant intervals.

In one of those long pauses, when silence itself, enhanced by contrast, seemed to become still deeper, a far different sound than the last I had been listening to caught my ear, – the sound of a loud but melancholy voice echoing through the arched avenues

of a vast garden, pronouncing distinctly these appalling words
– 'Judgment! judgment! tremble at the anger of an offended God!
Woe to Portugal! woe! woe!'

My hair stood on end – I felt as if a spirit were about to pass
before me; but instead of some fearful shape – some horrid
shadow, such as appeared in vision to Eliphaz, there issued
forth from a dark thicket, a tall, majestic, deadly-pale old man:
he neither looked about nor above him; he moved slowly on,
his eye fixed as stone, sighing profoundly; and at the distance of
some fifty paces from the spot where I was stationed, renewed
his doleful cry, his fatal proclamation: – 'Woe! woe!' resounded
through the still atmosphere, repeated by the echoes of vaults
and arches; and the sounds died away, and the spectre-like form
that seemed to emit them retired, I know not how nor whither.
Shall I confess that my blood ran cold – that all idle, all wanton
thoughts left my bosom, and that I passed an hour or two at my
window fixed and immovable?

Just as day dawned, I crept to bed and fell into a profound
sleep, uninterrupted, I thank Heaven, by dreams.

SEVENTH DAY

Morning.—The Prior of Batalha.—His Account of the Nocturnal
Wanderer.—A Procession.—Grand Façade of the Great
Church.—The Nave.—Effect of the golden and ruby light
from the windows.—Singularly devout celebration of High
Mass.—Mausoleum of John the First and Philippa.—Royal
Tombs.—The Royal Cloisters.—Perfect Preservation of this regal
Monastery.—Beautiful Chapter-house.—Tombs of Alphonso the
Fifth and his Grandson.—Tide of Monks, Sacristans, Novices,
&c.—Our Departure.—Wild Road.—Redoubled kindness of my
Reception by the Lord Abbot, and why.—Dr. Ehrhart's visit to
the Infirmary, and surgical raptures.—A half-crazed Poet and his
doleful tragedy.—Senhor Agostinho in the character of Donna
Inez de Castro.—Favouritism, and its reward.

9th June

A delightful morning sun was shining in all its splendour, when
I awoke, and ran to the balcony, to look at the garden and wild

hills, and to ask myself ten times over, whether the form I had seen, and the voice I had heard, were real or imaginary. I had scarcely dressed, and was preparing to sally forth, when a distinct tap at my door, gentle but imperative, startled me. The door opened, and the Prior of Batalha stood before me. 'You were disturbed, I fear,' said he, 'in the dead of the night, by a wailful voice, loudly proclaiming severe impending judgments. I heard it also, and I shuddered, as I always do when I hear it. Do not, however, imagine that it proceeds from another world. The being who uttered these dire sounds is still upon the earth, a member of our convent – an exemplary, a most holy man – a scion of one of our greatest families, and a near relative of the Duke of Aveiro, of whose dreadful, agonizing fate you must have heard. He was then in the pride of youth and comeliness, gay as sunshine, volatile as you now appear to be. He had accompanied the devoted duke to a sumptuous ball given by your nation to our high nobility: – at the very moment when splendour, triumph, and merriment were at their highest pitch, the executioners of Pombal's decrees, soldiers and ruffians, pounced down upon their prey; he too was of the number arrested – he too was thrown into a deep, cold dungeon: his life was spared; and, in the course of years and events, the slender, lovely youth, now become a wasted, care-worn man, emerged to sorrow and loneliness.

'The blood of his dearest relatives seemed sprinkled upon every object that met his eyes; he never passed Belem without fancying he beheld, as in a sort of frightful dream, the scaffold, the wheels on which those he best loved had expired in torture. The current of his young, hot blood was frozen; he felt benumbed and paralysed; the world, the court, had no charms for him; there was for him no longer warmth in the sun, or smiles on the human countenance: a stranger to love or fear, or any interest on this side the grave, he gave up his entire soul to prayer; and, to follow that sacred occupation with greater intenseness, renounced every prospect of worldly comfort or greatness, and embraced our order.

'Full eight-and-twenty years has he remained within these walls, so deeply impressed with the conviction of the Duke of Aveiro's innocence, the atrocious falsehood of that pretended conspiracy, and the consequent unjust tyrannical expulsion of the order of St. Ignatius, that he believes – and the belief of so pure and so devout a man is always venerable – that the horrors now perpetrating in France are the direct consequence of that event, and certain of being brought home to Portugal; which kingdom he declares is foredoomed to desolation, and its royal house to punishments worse than death.

'He seldom speaks; he loathes conversation, he spurns news of any kind, he shrinks from strangers; he is constant at his duty in the choir – most severe in his fasts, vigils, and devout observances; he pays me canonical obedience – nothing more: he is a living grave, a walking sepulchre. I dread to see or hear him; for every time he crosses my path, beyond the immediate precincts of our basilica, he makes a dead pause, and repeats the same terrible words you heard last night, with an astounding earnestness, as if commissioned by God himself to deliver them. And, do you know, my lord stranger, there are moments of my existence, when I firmly believe he speaks the words of prophetic truth: and who, indeed, can reflect upon the unheard-of crimes committing in France – the massacres, the desecrations, the frantic blasphemies, and not believe them? Yes, the arm of an avenging God is stretched out – and the weight of impending judgment is most terrible.

'But what am I saying? – why should I fill your youthful bosom with such apprehensions? I came here to pray your forgiveness for last night's annoyance; which would not have taken place, had not the bustle of our preparations to receive your illustrious and revered companions, the Lord Priors, in the best manner our humble means afford, impeded such precautions as might have induced our reverend brother to forego, for once, his dreary nocturnal walk. I have tried by persuasion to prevent it several times before. To have absolutely forbidden it, would have been harsh – nay, cruel – he gasps so piteously for air: besides, it might have been impious to do so. I have taken opinions in chapter upon this matter, which unanimously strengthen my conviction that the spirit of the Most High moves within him; nor dare we impede its utterance.'

I listened with profound seriousness to this remarkable communication; – the Prior read in my countenance that I did so, and was well pleased. Leading the way, he conducted me to a large shady apartment, in which the plash of a neighbouring fountain was distinctly heard. In the centre of this lofty and curiously-groined vaulted hall, resting on a smooth Indian mat, an ample table was spread out with viands and fruits, and liquors cooled in snow. The two Prelates, with the monks deputed from Alcobaça to attend them, were sitting round it. They received me with looks that bespoke the utmost kindness, and at the same time suppressed curiosity; but not a word was breathed of the occurrence of last night, – with which, however, I have not the smallest doubt they were perfectly well acquainted.

I cannot say our repast was lively or convivial; a mysterious gloom seemed brooding over us, and to penetrate the very atmosphere – and yet that atmosphere was all loveliness. A sky of intense azure, tempered by fleecy clouds, discovered itself between the tracery of innumerable arches; the summer airs (*aure estive*) fanned us as we sat; the fountain bubbled on; the perfume of orange and citron flowers was wafted to us from an orchard not far off: but, in spite of all these soft appliances, we remained silent and abstracted.

A sacristan, who came to announce that high mass was on the point of celebration, interrupted our reveries. We all rose up – a solemn grace was said, and the Prior of Batalha taking me most benignantly by the hand, the prelates and their attendants followed. We advanced in procession through courts and cloisters and porches, all constructed with admirable skill, of a beautiful grey stone, approaching in fineness of texture and apparent durability to marble. Young boys of dusky complexions, in long white tunics and with shaven heads, were busily employed dispelling every particle of dust. A stork and a flamingo seemed to keep most amicable company with them, following them wherever they went, and reminding me strongly of Egypt and the rites of Isis.

We passed the refectory, a plain solid building, with a pierced parapet of the purest Gothic design and most precise execution, and traversing a garden-court divided into compartments, where grew the orange trees whose fragrance we had enjoyed, shading the fountain by whose murmurs we had been lulled, passed through a sculptured gateway into an irregular open space before the grand western façade of the great church – grand indeed

– the portal full fifty feet in height, surmounted by a window of perforated marble of nearly the same lofty dimensions, deep as a cavern, and enriched with canopies and imagery in a style that would have done honour to William of Wykeham, some of whose disciples or co-disciples in the train of the founder's consort, Philippa of Lancaster, had probably designed it.

As soon as we drew near, the valves of a huge oaken door were thrown open, and we entered the nave, which reminded me of Winchester in form of arches and mouldings, and of Amiens in loftiness. There is a greater plainness in the walls, less panelling, and fewer intersections in the vaulted roof; but the utmost richness of hue, at this time of day at least, was not wanting. No tapestry, however rich – no painting, however vivid, could equal the gorgeousness of tint, the splendour of the golden and ruby light which streamed forth from the long series of stained windows: it played flickering about in all directions, on pavement and on roof, casting over every object myriads of glowing mellow shadows ever in undulating motion, like the reflection of branches swayed to and fro by the breeze. We all partook of these gorgeous tints – the white monastic garments of my conductors seemed as it were embroidered with the brightest flowers of paradise, and our whole procession kept advancing invested with celestial colours.

Mass began as soon as the high prelatic powers had taken their stations. It was celebrated with no particular pomp, no glittering splendour; but the countenance and gestures of the officiating priests were characterised by a profound religious awe. The voices of the monks, clear but deep-toned, rose pealing through vast and echoing spaces. The chant was grave and simple – its austerity mitigated in some parts by the treble of very young choristers. These sweet and innocent sounds found their way to my heart – they recalled to my memory our own beautiful cathedral service, and – I wept! My companions, too, appeared unusually affected; their thoughts still dwelling, no doubt, on that prophetic voice which never failed to impress its hearers with a sensation of mysterious dread.

It was in this tone of mind, so well calculated to nourish solemn and melancholy impressions, that we visited the mausoleum where lie extended on their cold sepulchres the effigies of John the First, and the generous-hearted, noble-minded Philippa; linked hand in hand in death as fondly they were in life. – This tomb is placed in the centre of the chapel.

Under a row of arches on the right, fretted and pinnacled and crocketed in the best style of Gothic at its best period, lie, sleeping the last sleep, their justly renowned progeny, the Regent Pedro Duke of Coimbra, whose wise administration of government, during the minority of his nephew and son-in-law Alfonso the Fifth, rendered Portugal so prosperous, and whose death, by the vilest treachery, on the field of Alfarubeira, was the fatal consequence of bitter feud and civil jealousies; the Infante, Dom John, a man of pure and blameless life; Fernando, whose protracted captivity in Africa was a long agony, endured with the resigned and pious fortitude of a Christian martyr; and Henry, to whom his country is beholden for those triumphant maritime discoveries, the result of his scientific researches unwearyingly pursued in calm and studious retirement.

All these princes, in whom the high bearing of their intrepid father, and the exemplary virtues and strong sense of their mother, the grand-daughter of our Edward the Third, were united, repose, after their toils and suffering, in this secluded chapel, which looks indeed a place of rest and holy quietude; the light, equably diffused, forms as it were a tranquil atmosphere, such as might be imagined worthy to surround the predestined to happiness in a future world.

I withdrew from the contemplation of these tombs with reluctance; every object in the chapel which contains them being so pure in taste, so harmonious in colour; every armorial device, every mottoed lambel, so tersely and correctly sculptured, associated also so closely with historical and English recollections – the garter, the leopards, the fleur-de-lis, 'from haughty Gallia torn;' the Plantagenet cast of the whole chamber conveyed home to my bosom a feeling so interesting, so congenial, that I could hardly persuade myself to move away, though my reverend conductors began to show evident signs of impatience.

The Prior of St. Vincent's observed to me, that as my Lord High Almoner expected us back to dinner, and had set his heart upon an *omelette à la provençale*, which he eagerly desired might be tossed up by my divine (as he was pleased to call him)

French cook, we had no time to lose. We were therefore hurried unmercifully through the royal cloisters, a glorious square of nearly two hundred feet, surrounded by most beautifully-proportioned arches, filled up with a tracery as quaint as any of the ornaments of Roslin chapel, but infinitely more elegant: it is impossible to praise too warmly their tasteful and delicate ramifications.

I could not fail observing the admirable order in which every – the minutest nook and corner of this truly regal monastery is preserved: not a weed in any crevice, not a lichen on any stone, not a stain on the warm-coloured apparently marble walls, not a floating cress on the unsullied waters of the numerous fountains. The ventilation of all these spaces was most admirable; it was a luxury to breathe the temperate delicious air, blowing over the fresh herbs and flowers, which filled the compartments of a parterre in the centre of the cloister, from which you ascend by a few expansive steps to the chapter-house, a square of seventy feet, and the most strikingly beautiful apartment I ever beheld. The graceful arching of the roof, unsupported by console or column, is unequalled; it seems suspended by magic; indeed, human means failed twice in constructing this bold unembarrassed space. Perseverance, and the animating encouragement of the sovereign founder, at length conquered every difficulty, and the work remains to this hour secure and perfect.

This stately hall, though appropriated to the official resort of the living, is also a consecrated abode of the dead. On a raised platform in the centre, covered with rich palls, are placed the tombs of Alfonso the Fifth, and his grandson, a gallant, blooming youth, torn from life, and his newly-married consort, the Infanta of Castile, and its fairest flower, at the early age of seventeen: with him expired the best hopes of Portugal, and of his father, the great John the Second.

My conductors, a great deal less affected than myself, would not allow me even one moment to ruminate and moralize upon vicissitudes and bereavements – they quite urged me along; and, to aid their active intentions, a tide of monks, sacristans, novices, seminarists, and the Lord knows who beside, appeared all of a sudden flowing forth from every cell and cloister: they had been all congregated, it seems, to do us honour and bid us adieu. The Prior, with his hands crossed on his breast, made me a low obeisance, and then opening his arms, gave me a cordial embrace.

Our army of attendants, mules, horses, and carriages, were all in waiting, ready drawn up at the same portal by which we had entered the night before. A grand interchange of salutations having taken place, we departed, the fatal voice, I verily believe, sounding in the ears of most of us – it certainly did in mine.

To dissipate impressions which hung heavily upon me, I asked permission of my illustrious companions to mount my horse, and to leave them to the ease and comfort of their capacious chaise; they *of course* returning by Aljubarota, and I by a short cut, over some of the wildest be-pined, and be-rosemaryed, and be-lavendered country I ever met with. Franchi, who was perfectly well acquainted with this wilderness, steered my course through all its mazes and straggling paths of sand and turf, alternately, bordered by the gum-cistus in full flaring flower, so strongly scented as almost to command me to go to sleep.

Dr. Ehrhart had taken his departure several hours before, charged with the important mission of conveying my culinary artist, the incomparable Monsieur Simon, to the longing arms of My Lord High Almoner; and, above all, by a vehement impulse to visit the infirmary of the convent, which he had been told contained an unusual number of patients, many of whom were afflicted with unusual disorders. This was attraction for him in an irresistible shape, and he most gladly left Batalha, and all its historical glories, (tombs, altars, and chapels, finished or unfinished,) to enjoy it.

I cannot describe in too glowing colours the increased jubilation with which I had the glory of being received by my Lord Abbot upon my return; for not only did he pass the threshold of his majestic portals to bid me welcome, but his principal confidant and factotum, the Sub-Prior, (whose strongly marked features were quite in the style of some of the finest studies of Masaccio,) assisted me to dismount, and condescendingly held my stirrup. From all these redoubled attentions, I plainly perceived that the wind had changed in my favour several points since yesterday: and what do you think had produced this agreeable alteration? – the *omelette à la provençale.*

'Oh, my dear, most excellent stranger!' – (my name for the time being had totally escaped him,) exclaimed his right reverence, 'what a treasure you possess in that admirable artist – o grande Simaõ! he has had the kindness to cast a new light over my stoves, – he is liberality itself; for, instead of locking up his knowledge, he has diffused it throughout my whole kitchen. Here –' continued he, pulling out some scrawls which Franchi had translated from the original French into very aboriginal Portuguese – 'Here are receipts, with marginal notes and illustrations, I mean to preserve, as carefully as I would a string of pearls, till my last hour. But, is it true, is it possible, you can be meditating to leave us so soon? Some bird of evil note whispered in my ear that you were determined to leave us tomorrow morning. Let me conjure you not to think of it: one day more, at least, do I pray and beseech you to bestow on us. My revered lords the Priors of Aviz and St. Vincent's have consented to comply with my request, subject to your approval – Oh do not refuse them and me!'

'Whatever your right reverence and my illustrious friends so earnestly desire cannot meet on my part with the slightest impediment,' answered I with a reverential obeisance.

'Now then,' rejoined the Prior, clapping his hands in ecstasy, 'we shall have that famous dish the admirable Simon promised me, – a macedoine, worthy of Alexander the Great; most happy, most grateful do I feel myself. But time is on the wing – let us profit whilst we can. I see you wish to refresh yourself by a change of dress in your own apartment: be it so – but don't be long; dinner shall be on table the moment you are ready; and you know, good becomes bad, in the case of dishes at least, if we wait a second beyond the auspicious time.'

Such logic was irresistible; I made all the haste required, and we sat down, I can truly say, to one of the most delicious banquets ever vouchsafed a mortal on this side of Mahomet's paradise. The macedoine was perfection, the ortolans and quails lumps of celestial fatness, and the sautés and bechamels beyond praise; and a certain truffle cream so exquisite, that my Lord Abbot forestalled the usual grace at the termination of repasts, most piously to give thanks for it.

The dinner was about half over, when in came Dr. Ehrhart in high spirits, rubbing his hands with triumphant glee, and talking to himself, as he was often wont, in the purest Alsatian. He had passed a couple of hours in the infirmary, and had visited all its closets of vials and gallipots. The drugs were not such (he informed us) either in quantity or quality as he could warmly commend; but the stock of maladies, to the alleviation of which they were destined, most ample. He had found a pretty sprinkling of complicated cases, – some highly curious, and, no doubt, *piquant*: one in particular, an ulcer of tremendous size, exhibited every freak Dame Nature was capable of playing upon such an occasion, – suppuration in one corner, callosity in another. He spoke of it in raptures, and regretted our stay was too limited to allow his committing to paper an exact delineation of this magnificent object in all its glow of colouring. He spoke handsomely also of the compound fracture of somebody's left leg. But when he came to the description of a sweet, simple perennial sore (simplex immunditiis), which had continued during a series of years to ebb and flow as regularly as the ocean, his enthusiasm knew no bounds. He said it was a most singular case – a beautiful case; a case so remarkable, so unprecedented, that he was determined all Europe should ring of it from side to side. He would throw his thoughts upon it into a dissertation of the length of at least sixty pages – that he would – and dedicate it to his native university. Then, bursting forth into a torrent of Latin, rendered unintelligible to all but the frequenters of Strasbourg or Colmar by the most villanous Alsatian twang, addressed himself point-blank to my Lord Abbot.

His right reverence, by no means pleased at being roused from the joys of the table by such an appeal and upon such a subject, very coolly replied, 'that he made it a rule never to speak or hear the Latin language out of the choir, if he could possibly help it.' This so palpable a rebuff silenced the good doctor, who had recourse to copious libations of generous wine to dispel the disappointment it occasioned; for he saw plainly that neither the fierce ulcer nor the gentle sore would meet with that attention from the supreme disposer of all things at Alcobaça, he was convinced they deserved so richly.

Notwithstanding the plastic effects of good cheer and flowing cups, my inestimable physician continued growling in an under tone during the whole remainder of our repast. And now the fullness of time for removing from the banquet-hall to the adjoining saloon being come, we repaired to another table, where all the delights of fruit and confectionary awaited us. Observing a good deal of whispering and message-sending between the Priors and their confidential attendants going forward, accompanied by nods and winks, I thought something particular for our special amusement was in contemplation; nor was I deceived: the agreeable little mystery was soon cleared up by the entrance of a tall, hook-nosed, sallow-complexioned personage, in a tarnished court suit; who advanced with measured strides, beating with one hand a slow and solemn tattoo upon a roll of parchment which he carried in the other.

I could not conceive what patent or document was about to be unfolded, when the personage giving the parchment a quick twirl with his bird-claw-like fingers, it displayed itself in the shape of a theatrical bill, engrossed in large characters flaming with vermilion and gold. On this scroll I read most distinctly that – this night, by the grace of God and the especial permission of the Abbot of Alcobaça, High Almoner of Portugal, &c. &c. &c. would be enacted the excruciating tragedy of Donna Inez de Castro, and the cruel murder of that lovely lady and her two innocent royal infants, represented on the stage: the part of Donna Inez by Senhor Agostinho José.

'The murder of the two royal infants!' exclaimed I; 'what means this? We know too well, alas! how the Lady Inez was disposed of; but her two sweet babes escaped from the fangs of the tyrant – did they not, my good Lord Abbot?'

'To be sure they did,' replied his right reverence: 'but this fine drama is not the production of one of our national bards; – an Italian gentleman, who has done us the honour of partaking of our hospitality for several years, and acquired in perfection our language, is the author; and, being a stranger, cannot be expected to feel so acutely for those precious infants as we Portuguese do: he therefore asked my leave to have them murdered, in order to add to the effect of the catastrophe: Rather than thwart a person of such transcendent abilities, and my very particular friend, I consented. He had half a mind to make them fall by their mother's own poniard in a fit of frenzy: but I could not allow of that; it would have been stretching a little too far – don't you think so?'

Recollecting the stretches I had often met with at home in historical novels, – witness Miss Lee's 'Recess' and many others – I made no objection, and turning to the bard, who was standing by wrapt into future murders, praised his sublime efforts in the tragic vein – the *terribile via* – in the most glowing terms I could muster. Animated by these grateful eulogies, he vociferated with dreadful vehemence, 'Let me but live a few years longer, and I will be the death of half the regal personages in the Portuguese history, after my own fashion and no other. I will slay them magnificently on the battle-field, though they died in their brocaded beds with all their courtiers puling around them; I will sink them in the ocean, though they expired on dry land; – their agonies in the act of drowning shall be horrible; – nay, more, I will call upon the Prince of the Morning, upon Lucifer himself, to bear them away for some secret sin or compact, though the prayers of the church had been exhausted to avert such a direful calamity.'

I thought this was a stretch with a vengeance: the Abbot, I plainly saw by his countenance, was of the same opinion; but, giving his ample shoulders a kind commiserating shrug (for the bard was a special favourite), contented himself with whispering to me – 'Sta doëdo – sta doëdo; the man's mad – all poets are.'

The Grand Prior of Aviz, who seemed to have no doubt of the truth of this observation in the present instance, looked at the bard with an expression of alarm that was almost ludicrous, and shrinking back in his chair, exclaimed piteously –

'What, Donna Inez and her children butchered upon the stage? I shall never be able to stand this; my eyes would become fountains, and we have had weeping enough lately,' (alluding perhaps to the liquefaction scene of last night:) 'tragedies of so deep a dye as this we are promised, affect my nerves in the most painful manner.' So saying, he retired without further ceremony, accompanied by two reverend fathers, dignitaries of the convent, who professed the same clerical aversion to scenes of bloodshed.

As soon as they had departed to a quiet game of voltarete

in their own snug quarters, the Lord Abbot, observing it was growing late, (for we had passed a most unconscionable time at table,) invited me to repair, under his Sub-Prior's guidance, to a theatre which had been temporarily fitted up in the most distant part of this immense edifice, of the extent of which, as well as of the endless variety of its cloistered galleries, cells, chapels, and chambers, I had not till this moment an adequate idea. Our peregrinations, therefore, were none of the shortest or least intricate. We passed through several galleries but feebly lighted, disturbing, I fear, the devotions of some aged monks, who were putting up their orisons before a lugubrious image of our Lady of the Seven Dolours, placed under a most sumptuously fringed and furbelowed canopy of purple velvet.

Farther on, another vast corridor branched off to that part of the convent allotted to scholars and novices. Not a few of these gentle youths were pursuing the study of the Jew's harp, and twanging away most proficiently. All these scudded off upon our approach, – the whole party had been at high romps, I suspect, from their flushed and blowzy appearance, – wishing us, I dare say, in purgatory, or a worse place, for having intruded, upon their recreations.

Advancing with due gravity, the valves of a lofty architectural door, with a pompous inscription on the pediment in golden characters, were unfolded, and we entered an extraordinarily spacious, coved saloon, which appeared to have been assigned to holier purposes, for there was an organ in a recess on one side of it. Across the whole end of this apartment was extended an immense green curtain, with the insignia of the convent emblazoned upon it in vivid colours; the centre of the saloon was occupied, as might have been expected, with many a row of polished oaken benches; but what I did not expect was an assemblage of more than one hundred venerable fathers, sitting in solemn ranks, as if they had been assisting at an ecumenical council, some wiping their spectacles, and some telling their beads. An effluvia, neither of jasmine nor roses – in short, that species of high conventual frowziness which monastic habits and garments are not a little apt to engender, affected my lay nerves most disagreeably.

The Prior of St. Vincent's, perceiving the uneasy curl up of my nose, whispered his neighbour, who whispered a second, who whispered a third, and presently a most grateful vapour of fragrant herbs and burnt lavender filled the room. Through its medium appeared descending from a portal, by a flight of most spacious steps, the Lord Abbot himself in grand costume. He insisted, with a positiveness which I could not avoid obeying, that I should take his abbatial chair next the orchestra, and placed himself on another equally ponderous, conceding the one on my right hand to the Prior of St. Vincent's.

We were no sooner settled, than half a-dozen sharp-toned fiddles, a growling bass, two overgrown mandolines, (lutes I suppose I ought to style them), and a pair of flutes most nauseously tweedled upon by two wanton-looking, blear-eyed young monks, who it would be charitable to suppose had caught cold at some midnight choral service, struck up a most singular and original species of antiquated overture. It was full of jerking passages in the style of 'Les Folies d'Espagne', and ended with a fugue that was catch-who-can in perfection.

Instead of the curtains drawing up at the conclusion of this strange musical farrago, there was a tedious pause, and I had full time to look round on the audience. Not five monks off my fauteuil, I caught the evil eye of Donna Francisca's director, sitting apart from the rest of the assembly, and looking more terrifically glum than any saint I ever beheld on an Italian sign-post, or in a German prayer-book.

I was trying to account for the delay of the performance, when sounds not unlike those which often proceed from a disturbed hen-roost became audible. Franchi's voice sounded predominant in this strange hubbub; and I found out afterwards that he had been fruitlessly attempting to persuade the Lady Inez (one of the most ungain hobbledehoys I ever met with) to abjure an enormous pair of jingling ear-rings, and to reduce a sweeping train he kept floundering over at every step, to the proportion of those in fashion amongst the tragedy queens of the Salitri theatre. Anything in the shape of metropolitan criticism wounded the awkward stripling's provincial amour-propre so deeply, that he threatened hysterics and an appeal to the Lord Abbot. This was conclusive; Franchi gave way, the Lady Inez retained her overflowing robes and her ear-rings, and the curtain rose.

Said his right reverence, whispering to me over the arm of

my ponderous chair, 'If you had heard Agostinho's declamation only two months ago, you would have been enchanted – his tones were so touching, so pathetic: his voice is now a little broken down; but you, who *have* an *ear*, will soon discover that it is on the high road of becoming a grand baritone: and as for his action, I am convinced you will soon allow nothing was ever more sublime.'

Just as I was on the point of replying to this warm encomium in a strain of correspondent eulogy, my Lord Abbot gently murmured, 'Hush, hush! don't you hear the Lady Inez?' I certainly did – and well I might, for a louder bellow was never given by the flower of any dairy. No cow bereaved of her last-dropped young one ever uttered sounds more doleful: they increased in depth and dismality, till the forlorn damsel, advancing to the lights on the stage, cried out, 'Cru-el, cru-el!' addressing, I suppose, the phantom of her redoubted father-in-law, 'and wouldst thou slay my innocents? Hast thou discovered my peaceful retirement? Where fly – where run?' She then continued, in a flow of at least one hundred lines, to picture her agonising fears, her dire presentiments, her frightful dreams; and, with looks that were meant to tear our feelings to the last tatter, she thus described her most terrific vision:

On thy wan disk, O pale and ghastly moon!
I saw portray'd a vengeful countenance;
And whilst upon it I did wildly gaze,
Methought it wore the semblance of the King –
(Now gelid horror claim'd me for her own.)
I tried to fly – I fled, but all in vain,
The dreaded face pursued me.
If I turn'd back, 'twas there; if I advanced,
The stern, cold image seem'd to freeze my soul,
Changing the genial current of my blood
Into a substance more severe than stone.
Avaunt, my hapless babes!
Approach me not,
Lest by some fatal petrifying power
Your limbs be fix'd in durance.

Donna Inez, by good luck, declaimed this magnificent piece of nonsense in a tolerably even key, and with really so just an emphasis, that the enraptured bard, laying aside his prompting-book, could not resist exclaiming, 'What do you think of that?' – 'E boa, e boa!' replied the Lord Abbot. And the whole assembly, both before and behind the scenes, re-echoed with one accord this favourable sentiment, and nothing but 'E boa, e boa!' was heard from one end of the saloon to the other.

Such universal encouragement did not fail to produce its effect upon Donna Inez, – rather too much so; for the higher notes of her semi-soprano voice having regained the ascendant, she squalled out of all mercy. My sense of hearing is painfully acute, and I hardly know what I would not have given for cotton to stop my ears with. However, they had soon a respite, Heaven be praised! the second act being totally employed by the plots and contrivances of the King and his counsellors, – quiet, chatty people, as loyal and complaisant as King Arthur's courtiers, Noodle, Doodle, and Foodle, in the incomparable tragedy of Tom Thumb.

In act the third, to my infinite astonishment, I found his majesty totally unacquainted with the little circumstance of Donna Inez having favoured his recreant son with a brace of children: he more than suspected espousals had taken place between them, but he little thought any fruits from the degrading match were in existence. Upon his prime counsellor's disclosing the fact, he asks with a perfidious coolness, 'What are they like?' – 'Doves, my dread lord,' answers the counsellor with infinite suavity: to which the infuriated monarch replies with a voice of thunder,

'It matters not, I'll tear their felon hearts –
PERISH THEY SHALL!'

And with this horrid menace quits the stage in a paroxysm of ungovernable fury, still repeating behind the scenes 'Perish they shall!' which was repeated again and again from the top of a ladder, by an old dignified monk, a passionate lover of the drama, but who being decorously shy of appearing on the open boards, had taken the part of Echo, which he performed to admiration.

Act the fourth offered nothing very loud or remarkable; but in act the fifth, horror and terror were working up to the highest pitch; two determined assassins had been procured – their looks most murderous – the children ran off – the assassins pursued – shrill and bitter squeakings were heard at the farthest extremity of the stage, such as a desperate conflict between rats or mice often produces behind old walls or wainscotings. The audience appeared prodigiously affected; most of them stood up, stretching out their necks like a flock of alarmed turkeys. This dreadful hurry-skurry ended by the first assassin's seizing the eldest infant by its beautiful hair, and tossing it apparently dead upon the stage. Three or four drops of pigeon's blood, squeezed out of some invisible receptacle, added a horrible appearance of reality to the foul deed.

It was now the other infant's turn to be murdered; and murdered it was, in a style that would not have disgraced one of Herod's best practitioners. The poor helpless innocent, who appeared to be most dreadfully frightened in right earnest, delivered its little dying speech with so much artlessness, that I was not surprised to see tears fall and hear sobs heave all around me. In short, affliction was almost exhausted to the last drop before Donna Inez was driven in, who, after calling to the sun, moon, and stars for vengeance, in accents at times most deep, at others most piercing, was immolated, by three distinct stabs of a poniard, upon the bodies of her children.

The deed so completely done, his most revengeful majesty, gloomier than Dis, and looking more truculent than ever the King of Judea was supposed to have done, entered with royal and stately step – stood gloating a minute or two over the horrid spectacle, and then, with the hoarse note of a carrion crow, croaked forth, 'I am satisfied.' The curtain fell; and putting aside its folds with a withered hand trembling with agitation, out issued the bard himself to speak an epilogue in his own character. It was tiresome and pompous enough, God knows, and concluded with a tirade, not exactly *à la Camoens,* pretty nearly as follows:

Lord of the firmament, couldst thou blaze on,
Urging thy coursers through the plains of light,
And not start back, affrighted at the deed!
Moon, veil thy orb – be quench'd, ye conscious stars,
Never again to sparkle as before!

Every soul in the assembly seemed to stand aghast, imprecating vengeance on the ruthless monarch, and feeling for the murdered innocents to their heart's core. Donna Inez was called for by my Lord Abbot, and embraced by his right reverence most blubberingly. The kind-hearted Prior of St. Vincent's wept aloud, – I tried my best, though in a lower key, to imitate him; the Poet was lauded to the skies, and received from the fountain-head of all good within these precincts something more solid than praise – a richly embroidered purse, heavy and chinking, which he deposited in one of his lank pockets, after making a grateful profound genuflexion.

'And now,' said my Lord Abbot, 'let us dry our tears and go to supper; and in order to give merit its just due, the Poet and Agostinho shall be of the party.' 'Why not?' said the Prior of St. Vincent's. 'Why not?' echoed I, – 'provided we have neither the king nor the murderers.'

As sunshine so frequently follows dark and drizzling weather, nothing could be more blithe or even frolicksome than our repast. The Grand Prior of Aviz, whom we found already placed near the hospitable board with his two card companions, talking over their game, congratulated himself warmly upon having escaped such a severe assault upon the pathetic feelings, and enjoyed the festivity of the moment without alloy. So we all did; and it was at a very late hour of one of the blandest summer nights I ever experienced that we retired to our apartments.

EIGHTH DAY

Too much of a good thing.—My longing for a Ramble.—Sage resolves.—A Gallop.—Pure and elastic Atmosphere.—Expansive Plain.—Banks of the River.—Majestic Basilica of Batalha.— Ghost-like Anglers.—Retrospections.—The Conventual Bells.— Conversation with the Prior.—A frugal Collation.—Romantic Fancies.—The Dead Stork and his Mourner.—Mausoleum of Don Emanuel.—Perverse Architecture.—Departure from Batalha.—Twilight.—Return to Alcobaça.

June 10

One may have too much of the good and grand things of this wicked world after all. I began to be tired of such perpetual gormandizing – the fumes of banquets and incense – the repetition of pompous rites – the splendour of illuminated altars and saints and madonnas, in fusty saloons, under still fustier canopies. My soul longed for an opener expanse – the canopy of the heavens. So I said to myself, 'Dr. Ehrhart may enjoy his infirmary; Franchi, his endeavours to introduce a purer taste of costume on the ruler of Alcobaça's temporary theatre; the Priors, their cards and their devotions; I will place the incomparable Simon at my Lord Almoner's uninterrupted disposal – they may toss omelets and season matelottes to their hearts' content, and, this being a day by courtesy entitled meagre, select the finest fish from their choicest reservoirs, if they so fancy. I pant like a hart for living waters: I am determined to follow the course of the river I noticed yesterday, winding its fresh sparkling stream between aromatic thickets; and should it lead me along its banks all the way to Batalha, so much the better. I have not seen half I wanted to see in that holy spot; and what little I did see floated before me like the shadows of a dream. I must be more intimately acquainted with the unfinished mausoleum of Don Emanuel, of which I have heard and read so much; – in short, I must breathe, which I can hardly be said to do in this too rich, too luxurious, too heavy atmosphere.'

These sage resolves being taken and communicated in due form to my right reverend companions, and by them to the ruling power of Alcobaça, (for I did not wish to disturb my Lord Abbot's slumbers, even with the good news of my having given up Monsieur Simon to his guidance,) I mounted my Arabian, patted his glossy neck, and whispering in his ear, 'Now we will repair to the desert – you will think of your native wilds, and I of mine,' off I galloped.

The fertile meadows and enclosures immediately round the convent were soon passed, and so were the chesnut woods hanging on the steeps crowned by the Moorish castle. My courser in full proof, pampered by the rich provender he had been so abundantly supplied with, set no bounds to his exertions, and I had hardly gained the level on the summit of the hills towards Aljubarota, before he fairly ran away with me. The country people, who, to do them justice, appeared very industriously employed, could not, however, help leaving their work to stare at the velocity of my scamper, distending their eyes as wide as they could possibly be distended when they beheld my Arabian on full stretch

'With flying speed outstrip the rapid wind,
And leave the breezes of the morn behind.'

The morn itself was most exhilarating: I never breathed in any atmosphere so pure or so elastic – it seemed to sparkle with life and light. The azure bloom investing the line of mountains which shelter Leiria was most beautiful. I longed to transfer their picturesquely varied outline to the leaves of my sketch-book; but it was in vain I wished to stop for that purpose – neither snaffle nor curb could arrest the speed of my courser.

At length, after a most inveterate gallop of at least five miles right ahead, persuasion effected what force was completely unequal to. He gave a lively, good-humoured, playful neigh, obeyed my much-loved voice, and halted. We were standing on an expanse of the smoothest sand, as firmly bound together as the nicest rolled walks of a regal garden; here and there patches of anemones and fragrant brushwood, cistus, lavender, and rosemary, varied the surface in irregular forms, like those of islands and continents distinctly defined on a map. No object afforded the smallest indication of human existence – neither the pointed roof of a shepherd's hovel, nor even a curling smoke. As far as the eye could reach, one uniform waste of level shrubs extended itself, bathed in the same equal purple light, and fanned by the same delightful air, impregnated with the same balsamic odour; an elysium without inhabitants, – unless, indeed, the souls of the departed were hovering about this serene and tranquil region, invisible to mortal eye.

Perhaps my Arabian beheld objects we are forbidden to gaze at; for he started and pawed the ground, and snorted with such vehemence that I almost expected every moment to see fire flash from his nostrils. By degrees this violent ferment subsided, and he became calm; what we superciliously call instinct seemed to point out to him that the region into which he had been pleased to carry me was totally barren of refreshment, and upon loosening his bridle, and allowing him to take what route he pleased, most prudently did he trace back his steps between entangled bushes, till I found myself under the shade of a forest of pine and chesnut, through which I descended to the margin of the river I so particularly wished to explore: and twenty times did I bless myself for having determined to follow the banks of this beautiful stream, the scenery they presented having a cast so novel and uncommon.

A broad path, or rather causeway, perfectly hard and dry, led me between a gigantic growth of canes, knotted like the bamboo; bulrushes of enormous size, and osiers, the tallest I had ever seen, waving their fresh green leaves high above my head, which they completely screened from the sun. The coolness they diffused, their incessant whispers, and the clear current of the river rippling among their stems, was so grateful both to the eye and ear, that I kept listening and lingering on, unwilling to emerge from this strange wilderness, and almost fancying I beheld one of those forests of weeds and grasses which, some five or six hundred thousand years ago, afforded refuge to a stupendous variety of monsters. Happily no icthyosaurus – no tortoise fifty feet in diameter, with paddles thrice as large as the helm of a first-rate man-of-war, oppressed me with their presence. I saw no living objects, except a shoal of fish, with scales as bright as silver, swiftly darting under the low arches formed by the luxuriant vegetation; and lizards as green as emeralds, ascending the sides of the causeway, and looking at me, I thought, with kind and friendly eyes.

For more than half a league did I continue along the path, hemmed in by aquatic plants of extraordinary vigour, springing from the richest alluvial soil. At length, just as I was beginning to think this world of reeds and osiers had no termination, the stream took a sudden bend, which I followed, and making the best of my way through every obstacle, escaped into an open space and open daylight. Right before me, at the extremity of an assemblage of hillocks, some bare, some covered with flowering heaths, but destitute of human or animal inhabitants, stood the lofty majestic basilica of Batalha, surrounded by its glorious huddle of buildings, from this point most picturesquely foreshortened. I could hardly believe so considerable and striking a group of richly parapeted walls, roofs, and towers, detached chapels, and insulated spires, formed parts of one and the same edifice: in appearance it was not merely a church or a palace I was looking at, but some fair city of romance, such as an imagination glowing with the fancies of Ariosto might have pictured to itself under the illusion of a dream.

Keeping my eyes fixed on a prospect which I tried to persuade myself partook less of the real than the visionary, I traversed an extensive level of sunburnt turf, and, on the other side of the hillocks bounding the lawn, again found myself on the banks of the river, which here presented the loveliest of mirrors – so calm, so pellucid, that I thought it a thousand pities no pleasanter objects were reflected from its surface, than a long line of ghost-like fathers, each with a fishing-rod projecting from his piebald drapery, angling on with pale and patient countenances. I did not perceive the melancholy prophet in this rank and file, – and I was not sorry; I dreaded to encounter his withering glance, to hear his foreboding voice; for I had been told he often pressed prophecies upon those least inclined to seek them; and I shrank from any knowledge of the horrors he might possibly disclose to me. Far from desiring to catch even the shadow of coming events, I said to myself, in the nervous language of Dryden,

Seek not to know what must not be reveal'd;
Joys only flow where fate is most conceal'd.
Too busy man would find his sorrows more,
If future fortunes he could know before;
For by that knowledge of his destiny,
He would not live at all, but always die.

Not above one hundred yards from the spot selected by the reverend fathers for their quiet recreation, the river, as if tired of being calm and placid, flowed with a brisker current, and rushing over a ledge of rocks, became all froth and foam. The light spray occasioned by its rapid movement refreshed the herbage on its banks so invitingly, that I leapt off my courser, and allowed him to profit as much as he pleased by the abundant pasture.

Throwing myself on the solid ground, I kept intensely poring over the stream, lost and absorbed in the train of interesting yet melancholy recollections which all that had occurred to me since I first entered this fair realm of Portugal was so well calculated to excite. I thought (alas! how vainly now!) of offers I had slighted with so much levity; of opportunities which, had they been grasped with a decided hand, might have led to happy results, and stemmed a torrent of evils. Since that period, the germ of destructiveness, which might then have been trodden down, has risen into a tree fraught with poisons, darkening the wholesome light, and receiving nourishment, through all its innumerably varied fibres, from the lowest depths of hell.

Whilst I was watching the constant flow of waters, and giving way to a tide of regrets in my own bosom equally ceaseless, the full rich tones of the conventual bells came booming over the watery levels – a summons the monks dared not disobey. Putting up their fishing-rods, they all dispersed in silence, with the exception of one, whom I joyfully recognised upon his nearer approach, and who seemed to feel equal pleasure in recognising me.

'To what lucky chance,' said the Prior, (for it was he who had advanced to me) 'are we indebted for the renewal of a visit I scarcely ventured to flatter myself would have taken place so soon?'

'To the genuine desire,' answered I, 'not only of assuring you once more of my real veneration, but a wish to examine the mausoleum of Don Emanuel, which I totally neglected in the hurry of yesterday – You remember how they pushed me along?'

He smiled; and I could not help thinking, from the cast of his countenance, that a few details of our Alcobara banquets and compotations would not have been ill received. Being, however, too discreet to tell tales out of this pious school, I said nothing of our gay supper, of my Lord Abbot's epicurean worship, of Monsieur Simon, or of the Poet, or of 'our tragedy,' or Senhor Agostinho, (ycleped Donna Inez), or of Donna Francisca's director, – though I had his cursed name on the tip of my tongue, ready to bolt out with not a few bitter animadversions upon a species of piety which had deprived me of many and many an hour of cheerfulness and joy.

Repressing, upon reflection, every spark of curiosity, as befitted a holy personage weaned from idle gossip, the good Prior most charitably observed, 'that my horse stood in need of more substantial refection than he could find on the river banks; and that, although he could not offer luxuries such as I had been accustomed to, the simple fare his far from wealthy convent afforded would be served up to me most gladly.'

Taking himself my horse by the bridle, he ushered me across the lawn into the same quadrangular cool and lofty chamber I had supped in before. A very youthful-looking lay brother received my Arabian into his charge with great delight, and stroked its mane and kissed its neck in a transport of childish fondness. As to me, though I was treated with less enthusiasm, there was no want of the utmost cordiality in my reception. An immense earthen platter, containing a savoury mess of fish and rice, vegetables delicately fried after the Italian fashion, caraffes of wine, baskets of ripe and fragrant fruit, pomegranates, apricots, and oranges, were neatly arranged on a marble table, having in its centre a rock of transparent ice, shining with ten thousand prismatic colours. To this frugal collation I sat down with the most sincere appetite, and was waited upon with hospitable glee by the angels of this wilderness – two lay brothers and as many novices, – all of whom appeared enchanted with an opportunity of making themselves of some use in this mortal existence. The Prior, crossing his hands on his bosom, entreated me to dispense with his attentions for half an hour, the choir service imperatively requiring his presence.

As soon as he had taken his departure, followed by his friars and novices, I gave myself wholly up to the enjoyment of those romantic fancies the surrounding scenery was so admirably well adapted to inspire. Two stately portals, thrown wide open to catch the breezes, admitted views of the principal courts and cloisters of this unequalled monument of the purest taste of the fourteenth century. A tranquil, steady sunlight overspread their grand broad surfaces. The graceful spire, so curiously belted with zones of the richest carved work, rose high above the ornamented parapets, relieved by a soft and mellow evening sky. None of the monks were moving about; but I heard with a sort of mournful pleasure their deep and solemn voices issuing from the great porch of the transept nearest the choir.

The young Egyptian-looking boys in white linen tunics I had noticed at my first visit were all at their accustomed avocations, dislodging every atom of dust from the deeply-indented tracery. The flamingo was there, but I missed the stork, – and knew but too soon the cause of his being missed; for, upon ascending the steps before the chapter-house, I discovered him lying stretched out upon the pavement stiff and dead. One of the boys stood bending over him in an attitude expressive of the deepest sorrow. The youth saw I compassionated him, and murmured out in a low desponding voice: 'This poor bird followed me all the way from my home in Alemtejo – a long distance from Batalha. He was the joy of my life, and dearly loved by my mother, who is dead. I shall never see her again in this world, nor hear the cheering cry of this our fond household bird, calling me up in the morning: he will receive no more crumbs from my hand – he will keep faithfully by my side no longer. I have no one now in this grand place who loves me!' And he burst into a flood of bitter tears, and it was a relief to my own heart – a great relief – to join in his mourning.

The Prior, who happened to come up at the moment, could not at first imagine what had affected me; but when I pointed to the boy and the lifeless stork, he entered into my feelings with his characteristic benevolence, and spoke words of comfort to the poor weeping child, with such true parental kindness as seemed to assure him he had still a friend. Touched to the heart, the boy fell on his knees, and kissed the pavement and his stork at the same time. I left him extending his arms to the good Prior in an act of supplication, which I learnt afterwards had not been treated with cold indifference.

And now the Prior, with his wonted solemn and courteous demeanour, offering to be himself my guide to the mausoleum of Don Emanuel, we traversed a wilderness of weeds, – this part of the conventual precincts being much neglected, – and entered a dreary area, surrounded by the roofless, unfinished cluster of chapels, on which the most elaborately sculptured profusion of ornaments had been lavished, as often happens in similar cases, to no very happy result. I cannot in conscience persuade myself to admire such deplorable waste of time and ingenuity – 'the quips, and cranks, and wanton wiles' of a corrupt, meretricious architecture; and when the good Prior lamented pathetically the unfinished state of this august mausoleum, and almost dropped a tear for the death of Emanuel its founder, as if it had only occurred a week ago, I did not pretend to share his affliction; for had the building been completed according to the design we are favoured with by that dull draftsman Murphy, most preciously ugly would it have been; – ponderous and lumpish in the general effect, exuberantly light and fantastic in the detail, it was quite a mercy that it was never finished. Saxon crinklings and cranklings are bad enough; the preposterous long and lanky marrow-spoon-shaped arches of the early Norman, still worse; and the Moorish horse-shoe-like deviations from beautiful curves, little better.

I have often wondered how persons of correct taste could ever have tolerated them, and batten on garbage when they might enjoy the lovely Ionic so prevalent in Greece, the Doric grandeur of the Parthenon, and the Corinthian magnificence of Balbec and Palmyra. If, however, you wish to lead a quiet life, beware how you thwart established prejudices. I began to perceive, that to entertain any doubts of the supreme excellence of Don Emanuel's scollops and twistifications amounted to heresy. Withdrawing, therefore, my horns of defiance, I reserved my criticisms for some future display to a more intelligent auditor, and chimed in at length with the Prior's high-flown admiration of all this fillagree, and despair for its non-completion; so we parted good friends. My Arabian was brought out, looking bright and happy; I bade a most grateful adieu to the Prior and his attendant swarm of friars and novices, and before they had ceased staring and wondering at the velocity with which I was carried away from them, I had reached a sandy desert above a mile from Batalha.

Night was already drawing on – the moon had not yet risen – a dying glow, reflected from the horizon above the hills, behind which the sun had just retired, was thrown over the whole landscape. 'Era già, l'hora' – it *was* that soothing, solemn hour, when by some occult, inexplicable sympathy, the interior spirit, folded up within itself, inclines to repel every grovelling doubt of its divine essence, and feels, even without seeking to feel it, the consciousness of immortality.

The dying glow had expired; a sullen twilight, approaching to blackness, prevailed: I kept wandering on, however, not without some risk of being soon acquainted with the mysteries of a future world; for had not my horse been not only the fleetest, but the surest of foot of his high-born tribe, he must have stumbled, and in dangerous places, for such abounded at every step. As good fortune would have it, all the perils of the way were got over; the grand outline of the colossal monastery and its huge church emerged from the surrounding gloom; innumerable lights, streaming from the innumerable casements, cast a broad gleam over the great platform, where my Lord Almoner and his guests were walking to and fro, enjoying the fresh evening air, and waiting my return, they were pleased to say, with trembling anxiety.

The first question I was asked upon entering the grand illuminated saloon was, how I had fared, and whether I did not feel half-dead for want of refreshment. 'We, for our parts,' exclaimed my Lord Abbot, 'have been the happiest of the happy: your great Simon has surpassed even my expectations. And now, to another proof of his transcendent skill, – now to supper.'

NINTH DAY

Lamentations on our Departure, and on the loss of Monsieur Simon.—Mysterious Conference.—A sullen Adieu.—Liveliness of the Prior of St. Vincent's.—Pleasant Surprise.—Vast and dreary Plain.—A consequential Equerry.—An Invitation.—The Bird-Queen.—Fairy Landscape.—The Mansion.—The great Lady's Nephews.—Reception by her Excellency.—Her attendant Hags.—The great Lady's questions about England and dismal ideas of London.—The Cuckoo.—Imitations.—Dismay of her Sublime Ladyship and her Hags.—Our Departure from the bird-ridden Dominions.—Cultivated Plain.—Happy Peasantry, and their gratitude to the Monks of the Royal Convent.—Their different feelings towards the great Lady.—Female Peasants bearing Offerings to our Lady of Nazare.—Sea View.—Pedraneira.—Banquet of Fish.—Endless Ravine.—Alfagiraõ.—Arrival at the Caldas.—Sickly Population.—Reception of Dr. Ehrhart.—His Visit to the Invalids, and contempt of the Medical Treatment of the place.—A determined Bore—His Disaster.

June 11th

Great were the lamentations in Alcobaça when the hour of our departure arrived, – a voice of wailing scarcely equalled in Rama when Rachel wept for her lost children. Here, I am perfectly convinced, that had my Lord Abbot been permitted, like spiritual lords in our own country, to avow the legal paternity of a dozen brats, he would sooner have spared the whole treasure than have lost the advice and exertions of a being he venerated above all others without any exception – a matchless cook. It was a cruel separation: the artist himself, who had a susceptible heart, as well as a hand gifted with the most exquisite sauce-making sensibilities, was far from being callous to the raptures of such a discriminating gourmand as the ruler of Alcobaça. To remain in this holy place, to quit my service, I verily believe never entered the head beneath his milk-white betasseled cook-cap; but he was visibly moved by the rapturous eulogies, still more perhaps by the generous presents I suspect he had received; he saw with great commiseration how acutely the Lord Abbot felt his departure. Pity, we all know, melts the heart to love, and love full often to devotion; so, when we repaired, one and all, to take a parting mass before setting out on our journey, Monsieur Simon, though little given to demonstrations of piety, fell to thumping his breast with such vehemence, that I could not resist saying to him as we came out of church, 'Simon, my Lord Abbot seems to have quite reconverted you; you are becoming astonishingly religious.' – 'Ah, Monsieur,' said he, 'on le sera, à moins; Monseigneur rend la réligion si aimable.'

I thought now, as the equipages, horses, &c. were all marshalled before the grand entrance, we were actually ready to set out. No such thing: the Grand Prior of Aviz, taking me aside for a moment, whispered in my ear that he had still a few words of great importance in store for my Lord Almoner, and begged me to cast another look at my favourite portrait of St. Thomas of Canterbury whilst he delivered them.

Calling his colleague of St. Vincent's, they both entered a private room of audience adjoining the hall of pictures, from which my Lord Almoner had not yet stirred; and notwithstanding the doors had been immediately closed, I heard a loud storm of indistinct but angry words approaching to tempest, the exact import of which it is not in my power to reveal, supposing I had the inclination; but I learned afterwards (though rather vaguely) from one of the Prior of St. Vincent's confidants, that they related to certain mysteries, certain despotic imprisonments, certain grotto-like communications, between this sacred asylum and another not less monastic, though tenanted by the fairer portion of holy communities – the daughters of prayer and penitence.

Providence, that tempers the wind to the shorn lamb, and does kind things now and then to pets and favourites, was not totally ungracious to my Lord Almoner upon this occasion. Had it not, by directing the semi-inquisitorial visit of the two prelatical missionaries, given his right reverence of Alcobaça's thoughts serious occupation, they might have dwelt far more painfully upon the departure of his beloved Simon: the sharp edge of his afflictions in this particular was taken off by the reflections which the late stormy conference had inspired.

When he came forth to accompany us to our carriages, as the rules of courtesy demanded, I observed a marked change in his deportment and countenance; there were no longer those sunny smiles, those cooings and chucklings, which had greeted my revered companions upon their arrival. A sullen, sulky gloom – a but half-subdued expression of anger pervaded his every look and gesture: coldly and formally, therefore, did we take our leave. Not above half of the community were drawn out in complimentary array, and that half looked strange and suspicious, as if they conjectured something had happened unpleasant and awkward. The two fathers deputed to attend us to Pedraneira got into one of their heavy conventual vehicles, and, in their capacities of conductors, led the van. I looked back as we drove off; and, there stood my Lord Almoner, with his eyes fixed on the pavement, before the grand portal, immovable, and as if he had been turned to stone.

The Grand Prior of Aviz having something very confidential to discuss with his secretary, begged me to excuse his accompanying me in my carriage: the Prior of St. Vincent's took his place; an exchange I had no cause to complain of, his conversation being so full of hilarity and life. This flow of cheerful good spirits did not, however, carry him beyond the limits of the most perfect discretion: not a syllable that had the slightest reference to pains or pleasures below ground escaped his lips – not the smallest hint – no, not a breath.

All attempts to gain information upon this curious point proving fruitless, we praised fine weather and fine prospects, and deprecated bad roads. We had no occasion, however, to do so; for scarcely had we turned the angle of one of the vast walled enclosures belonging to the convent, and expected to sink into some frightful rut or sandy furrow, when an immense body of well-clothed peasants, with their strong bright tools slung over their sturdy shoulders, met us with loud *vivas,* and the tranquillizing assurance that the whole way to Pedraneira had been smoothed by their exertions: so we rolled along over firm gravel and compact heath-faggots most delightfully.

We soon reached the banks of my favourite river, and crossed over a very picturesque-looking bridge, without parapets, to its opposite shore – a vast and dreary plain. We were beginning to experience the effects of heat rather oppressively, when we entered a forest of pine, and felt much invigorated by fragrant, genial breezes, – shade was out of the question, most of the trees being tall and sapless.

In one of the least frequented parts of this superannuated forest, the career of our caravan was suddenly arrested by a most imposing cocked-hatted personage, booted up to the chin, like West's heroes in his picture of the Battle of the Boyne, bestriding a managed horse, decked out in all the pride of burnished pistol and gold-laced holster.

This most consequential of equerries, with as much solemnity as if he had been reading a state proclamation, invited us, in the name of his mistress, a lady of high caste and importance, to screen ourselves from the meridian heats in her quinta hard by; a most blessedly shady place, in which she had congregated, I verily believe, half the birds in the country – those least in repute, such as kites, owls, and buzzards, not excepted.

My Lord of Aviz was still too deeply engaged in confidential discourse with his secretary to much relish making a halt and getting out of his carriage; but the Prior of St. Vincent's and myself were perfectly disposed to accept the invitation, having learnt, during our course of Alcobaça gossip, too many curious particulars about this eminent lady-patroness of the feathered tribe, not to feel extremely curious to be admitted into the penetralia of the asylum she afforded them; a favour rarely granted, and which sprang most probably out of a strong curiosity to see and fondle my beloved Arabian, not my own dear self

– her most excellent ladyship professedly not caring one pip of an orange for strangers of any description or quality, unless they were blessed with four feet, or a natural mantle of feathers.

Preceded by the right pompous and fustified equerry, we diverged from the mended track into an avenue of dwarfish cork-trees, leading straight to a lofty wall, which extended far to the right and left of a grand massive Tuscan gateway. The wide space before this stately entrance exhibited the refreshing sight of marble troughs brimful of the clearest water; heaps of oats and barley, amply sufficient to supply the wants of our mules; and paniers of bread and oranges, under very substantial canvass awnings.

My reverend companions, as in duty bound, went immediately to offer their homage to the bird-queen; but I begged to be excused for the moment, promising that as soon as my Arabian had been refreshed and brightened up by a good rubbing, I would lead him myself to the foot of the throne of these dominions. Having gained this respite, the whole party dispersed as seemed best in their eyes, and I entered perfectly alone the deeply shaded inclosure – without exception one of the strangest scenes of fairy-land ever conjured up by the wildest fancy.

As far as the eye could stretch, extended a close bower of evergreens, myrtle, bay, and ilex, not to mention humble box, lofty, broad, and fragrant; on either side, arches of verdure most sprucely clipped, opened into large square plats of rare and curious flowers; and in the midst of each of these trim parterres, a fountain enclosed within a richly-gilded cage, containing birds of every variety of size, song, and plumage; parroquets with pretty little flesh-coloured beaks, and parrots of the largest species, looking arch and cunning, as they kept cracking and grinding walnuts and filberts between their bills as black as ebony.

In one of these enclosures I noticed an immense circular basin of variegated marble, surrounded by a gilt metal balustrade, on which were most solemnly perched a conclave of araras and cockatoos. Their united screechings and screamings upon my approach gave the alarm to a multitude of smaller birds, which issued forth in such clouds from every leaf and spray of these vaulted walls of verdure, that I ran off as if I had committed sacrilege, or feared being transformed by art-magic into a biped completely rigged out with beak, claws, and feathers.

The strange green light which faintly pervaded the closely-bowered alleys – the aromatic odour universally diffused – the rustle of wings, the chirping and twittering above my head and on every side of me, was so completely bewildering and magical, that I almost doubted whether ever again I should be permitted to emerge into common life or common daylight. The soft, perfumed, voluptuous atmosphere of this seemingly enchanted garden, induced a languor and listlessness to creep over me I scarcely ever felt before.

Just as I was giving way to this gentle indolence, and had sunk down by the marble basin soothed by the bubblings of its little quiet jet-d'eau, I heard the heavy tramp of the solemn equerry, – and there he was true enough. 'Be pleased, sir,' said he, making a bow which the stiffest and most formal dancing-master of the days of Louis the Fourteenth would have gloried in, – 'be pleased to comply with the urgent request of my Lord Prior of Aviz, who is waiting with impatience to have the honour of presenting you to my most illustrious and most excellent mistress.'

'Oh!' answered I, 'by all means; nothing less than the attractions of your most illustrious and most excellent lady's feathered favourites could have detained me from her presence – pray lead me to it.'

The way was not long, but most delightful, under a continued arbour of exotic plants, looking as healthful as if they had been quite at home in Portugal – born and bred there for centuries. On either side, more flowerbeds, and more birds, some at liberty and some in cages.

The house itself, at which we arrived in due course, though of an extent quite remarkable, was far from presenting a palace-like appearance, being in height only one story. Its verandas, however, commanded respect: they were extremely spacious, paved and balustraded with marble.

Under the terraces they supported, were offices innumerable, not unlike rabbit-burrows in the realm of Brobdignag, out of, and into which, were continually creeping a great number of tawny-coloured menials, very slightly clothed indeed, all busily engaged in tending the feathered race committed to their charge: for half these burrows, or arched chambers, or whatever we please to call them, were closed with light trellises of wire, forming, after all, no very pleasant aviaries. Certain most horribly discordant screechings, which pierced my ears every now and then, seemed to indicate that the birds of the establishment were not so happy or judiciously governed as their sovereign mistress imagined – the case of subjects in most dominions.

On the lowest step of a grand flight of steps leading up to the principal veranda, stood three young gentlemen, aged fourteen, fifteen, and sixteen years, the nephews of the great lady, as like one to the other as if they had been not only twins, but triplets; all sleek, and smooth, and sallow; all dressed in obsolete court-dresses of blue and silver tissue, each with his powdered hair in a silken bag, each with his little cut-steel-hilted sword, and each with a little abdominal bulge that promised in the course of a very few years to become a paunch of considerable dignity. In close attendance upon these hopeful youths, were a stripling page, a half-crazed buffoon, an ex-jesuit, and a dwarf; personages indispensable to a noble and well-constituted Portuguese establishment. Down went all their heads the moment I drew near, and down went mine to the very earth in return for so much courtesy.

We ascended the steps all together right lovingly, the three youths marching hand-in-hand. Nothing could exceed the decorous behaviour of these sweet young gentlemen; it did honour to their preceptor, who had brought them up in the most commendable fear of the devil and of taking birds' nests; – the latter, of all crimes, was esteemed the most heinous in those dominions.

Independently of my fondness for brute animals, I am not unapt, cameleon-like, to take the colour of what happens to pass around me. It might be supposed, therefore, that I entered fully into the fashion of the place, and expressed my fondness and admiration of every species of bird it had pleased God in his infinite goodness to create, with enthusiasm. So disposed, and in this blessed trim, I entered the grand saloon of the great lady's residence. Her excellency was seated at its upper end in a high-backed wicker chair, stuck close to the wall. Seven or eight old hags, of a most forbidding aspect, all in black, and all more sincerely bearded, I make no doubt, than the Countess Trifaldi's attendants, were ranged to the right and left, on narrow benches; forming one of the ugliest displays of living tapestry my eyes had ever encountered.

The two Priors, who, to their no great delight, one may easily imagine, formed part and parcel of this odious assembly, had reserved a wicker chair, the coolness of which was completely neutralized by a red velvet cushion, for the stranger – the unhappy stranger, who felt already quite sufficiently annoyed and sweltered.

As soon as we had exchanged an infinity of salutations, and several capacious golden snuff-boxes had gone their rounds with as much regularity as the planets, four antiquated damsels entered the presence, bearing trays, heaped high with candied apricots and oranges, and, still sweeter than all the sweetmeats ever confectionized, a preparation of the freshest eggs ever laid, with the richest sugar ever distilled from the finest canes ever grown in the Brazils for private consumption under the most skilful management.

To these succeeded another entree of ci-devant young women, who presented us, upon embossed silver salvers, goblets of cut glass, containing the coldest and purest water.

Right opposite to where we sat, formally marshalled all of a row, the young fidalgos and their preceptor, who had enlisted Doctor Ehrhart, Franchi, and the two Priors' secretaries into their ranks, were seated on stools, not in the least superior either in shape or dimensions to those used for milking in the homeliest bartons of our own dear farming country.

It was some time before any sounds, except the whirring and whizzing of enormous cockchafers, and the flirting of fans almost as large as the vans of a windmill, were audible. At length the great lady broke silence, by asking me whether we had any birds in England: to which, rising from my chair, I replied with a low obeisance, that, thanks be to God, we were blessed with an immense number.

'Indeed!' rejoined her excellency; 'I thought your country too cold to allow them, sweet dears, to build their nests and enjoy themselves.'

'Yes,' observed the Jesuit, 'the climate of your island must be very bitter. Camoens, whose authority none can dispute, calls it

A grande Inglaterra che de neve
Boreal sempre abunda.'
(Canto 6, stanz. 42.)

'Which being undoubtedly the case,' continued the bird-queen, 'that great number you boast of must be imported: indeed, I understood as much from an old servant of my father's, who made a fortune by dealing in Canary-birds, and taking them to your great town, where you can hardly distinguish night from day, as he told me. But what will not the lure of gain make us submit to? He was continually resorting to that black place with his living wares, (how I pity them!) and, to be sure, he gained sufficient, though he almost coughed his lungs out, to buy a nice quinta in my neighbourhood. He is an excellent judge of everything that concerns birds; knows how to treat them in moulting-time, which few do; and for the sagacity with which he discovers an incipient pip, and stops its progress, I may venture to affirm from long experience, he has no equal. But tell me fairly, most estimable Englishman, have you any native birds in your island?'

'Yes, madam,' was my triumphant reply, 'we have; one in particular – seldom seen, but often heard – the cuckoo.'

I had scarcely pronounced that name, when an exact imitation of its well-known sound burst forth from Franchi and the buffoon, who was standing behind his stool, to the high glee of the young gentlemen, their page and dwarf, and the evident dismay of her sublime ladyship and her hags in waiting. They looked as if they could have pinched us all as sharply as the snuff in their ample boxes. In short, surprise and anger at Franchi's want of decorum, and a suspicion, perhaps, of being what we call quizzed, in our vernacular slang, began to manifest itself; when the solemn equerry announced with his wonted solemnity, that our carriages were in waiting, and my Arabian at the door, ready to receive the honour of a caress from his most illustrious and excellent mistress.

Overjoyed at this intelligence, the two Priors and myself, all heartily tired of our formal sitting, rose up without a moment's delay; so did the great lady, and her train of hags and dismal damsels, following each other one by one. As soon as this dolorous procession reached the gateway, a great number of gigantic dark-brown umbrellas were spread forth, and under their deep shade my astonished courser, with his fine arched neck held down by a couple of grooms, was patted in succession by the lank, cold fingers of the bird-queen and her antiquated attendants then, followed as many curtseys, and as low as the dry stiff knees that performed them could contrive to drop; and the Grand Prior of Aviz signifying that he had no further occasion for the attendance of his confidential secretary, I got into his dormeuse, ordered my Arabian to follow, and bade, I hope and trust, an eternal adieu to this region of screaming birds, clipped hedges, and sour-visaged old women.

It was some time before we cleared the walls of these bird-ridden dominions, a great deal more extensive than I apprehended. Our route, distinctly marked out by its recent mendings, led us across a plain in the highest state of cultivation, forming a most agreeable contrast to the ragged weather-beaten forest and pompous idle inclosure we had left behind. Here every object smiled; here every rood of land was employed to advantage, the Lombard system of irrigation being perfectly understood and practised. Every cottage, apparently the abode of industrious contentment, had its well-fenced garden richly embossed with gourds and melons, its abundant waterspout, its vine, its fig-tree, and its espalier of pomegranate.

The peasantry, comfortably clad in substantial garments, looked kindly and unenviously at our splendid caravan, because their hearts were expanded by good treatment, their granaries amply stored, their flocks numerous and healthy, and their landlords, the rich monks of Alcobaça, neither griping nor tyrannical. When the Prior of Aviz stopped to converse with these good people, which he frequently did, and inquired with his usual affable benignity, 'Who taught you to till your land so neatly? to manure it with so much judgment? to raise such crops of grain? to spare your cattle all forced oppressive labour? to treat their young with so much gentleness?' the answer was prompt and uniform, – 'Our indulgent masters and kind friends, the monks of the royal monastery.'

The pleasure my excellent friend received from this communication beamed forth from his ingenuous countenance, as he noted down the result of his inquiries on his tablets; a set-off, perhaps, in his opinion, to the strange mysterious report he had received of certain unedifying frailties. Whatever snares of the evil-one my kind hosts of Alcobaça may have fallen into beneath ground, few communities ever conferred more solid benefits upon its surface to all their dependants.

Very different were the replies to our queries about the great lady: shrugs of the shoulder, and shakings of the head, gave us to understand most plainly, that, as far as her territorial influence extended, – luckily small in comparison with that of the great convent – it was of a nature more blighting than genial, less charitable than oppressive. And as to her birds, they were a flagrant nuisance – whole flights of her doves, parrots, kites, finches, and thrushes being allowed to commit with the most perfect impunity every species of depredation best suited to their habits and propensities.

We were all so enchanted with these scenes of rural delight and joy, that we ordered our carriages not to be driven along too rapidly. We had to pass the river again and again over the same sort of ruinous bridges as we had met with in the immediate vicinity of Alcobaça. My revered companion could not repress sensations of terror as we jolted up and down steep arches unprotected by any parapet – sensations which the most fervid exhortations on my part to put faith in Saint Anthony could not subdue; so out he trundled into all the dust and offal of the road.

After not less than three or four of these rather dangerous transits, we mounted a heathy, pastoral hill, browsed by goats, and met a long string of female peasants, bearing offerings of various kinds to our Lady of Nazaré; and presently the sanctuary, to which they were going in pilgrimage, discovered itself on the brow of a craggy eminence shelving down to the Atlantic.

Much praise cannot in truth be lavished upon this edifice, which is neither considerable nor picturesque; but the colours of the wide unlimited ocean, so pure, so vivid, so beautifully azure, made up for all other deficiencies, and, joined to the reviving freshness of the sea-breeze, gave my spirits the most delightful and animated flow. Gay, agile, and buoyant, I leaped out of the carriage the moment it stopped, and was immediately received into the arms and garlick-scented embrace of the two aged fathers, our harbingers, who had preceded us to Pedraneira.

This most opulent farm-mansion, the capital of the conventual domains in these quarters, had very much the air of an oriental caravanserai, with stables for mules and courts surrounded with arches, castellated granaries, and vaulted chambers, incrusted with clean glossy tiles, by no means indifferently painted with scriptural and legendary subjects. In the largest and coolest of these apartments we were regaled with a magnificent banquet of fish, caught near the rocks of Peniche, and reckoned the best upon the whole line of the coast.

Being a fast-day, except a few hashes of pork for heretics, savoury as the flesh-pots of Egypt, nothing unorthodox was served up. Dr. Ehrhart, however, partook of every ragout set before him indiscriminately, to the scandal of our hosts, the monks and their attendants. All the rest of the company having made their election, stuck to fish with true Catholic propriety.

Our repast quickly dispatched, and the aged fathers most kindly thanked and most willingly dismissed from their attendance, – for, to say truth, they were not only intolerably effluvient but inveterately prosy, – we made haste to set forth in order to reach the Caldas before night. As long as we continued on the shore enjoying the vast marine prospect and the unceasing sound of the waves, nothing could be pleasanter; but when we entered an almost endless ravine, its banks entirely covered with the strong healthy flowers of the *Papaver corniculatum*, our progress was slow and tedious. To this ravine succeeded another, diversified by a more agreeable sort of vegetation – the yellow lupin in all its fragrance.

At some distance we saw a Moorish castle, standing proudly on an insulated eminence, presenting a grand mass: it bears also a grand name, Alfagiraõ. This picturesque object, the stillness and soft hues of evening, and the perfume of the lupins, were circumstances too pleasing not to make us regret our arrival at the Caldas with quite sufficient light to distinguish all its ugliness; – its dull monotonous houses, with their coarse green window-blinds and shutters flapping to and fro in the dusty breeze; and its heavy verandas, daubed over with yellow ochre, and striped in places with blue and red, in patterns not unworthy of Timbuctoo or Ashantee.

In my eyes, the whole of this famous stewing-place wore a sickly unprepossessing aspect. Almost every third or fourth person you met was a quince-coloured apothecary, accoutred like a courtier on his march to the drawing-room, and carrying many a convenient little implement in a velvet bag, as pompously as if he had been a lord chancellor; and every tenth or twelfth, a rheumatic or palsied invalid, with his limbs all atwist, and his mouth all awry, being conveyed to the baths in a chair. You could hardly move without running your head against the voluminous wig of some medical professor, and hearing the formidable stump of his gold-headed cane.

The news of the advent of a great German doctor, ex-physician to the household of his ex-majesty the most Christian King, soon spread itself throughout the Caldas; and we had not set our feet on the hot flag-stones of this physical emporium above five or six minutes, before a deputation of the faculty arrived. These sages came on purpose to introduce themselves to Dr. Ehrhart, and entreat the honour of his company on a professional tour to their principal patients. His account of the woeful condition and appearance of the wretched invalids in their respective tubs and cisterns, related in Alsatian French, sound Latin, and broken Portuguese, was most original.

'I found many of them,' said the indignant doctor, 'with galloping pulses, excited almost to frenzy by the injudicious application of these powerful waters, and others with scarcely any pulses at all. The last will be quiet enough ere long; and considering what dreadful work these determined Galenists drive amongst them, with their decoctions, and juleps, and spiced boluses, and conserve of mummy, and the devil knows what, I expect a general gaol-delivery must speedily take place, and the souls of these victims of exploded quackeries be soon released from their wretched bodies, rendered the worst of prisons by a set of confounded bunglers.'

Never shall I forget the indignant scowl my angry doctor cast upon the contemners of simple and vegetable medicine. His ebullitions of wrath remained unpacified till he had swilled down the contents of an ample caraffe of wine, diluted with only a very few drops of water, accompanied by a platter of those savoury bulbs which geese are so often stuffed with in England, for the express purpose, he openly avowed, of decreasing flatulence, and expelling the prince of the air and all his satellites. I thought the Prior of St. Vincent's would never have ceased laughing at this species of exorcism. The Portuguese have in general a strong relish for coarse practical jokes; and I am far from pretending that this one was not most decidedly of the number.

The master and mistress of the large rambling habitation assigned to us thought proper to light up with their own hands all the tapers in the Bohemian glass sconces and chandeliers of the barn-like saloon on their ground-floor. Such a glare, equal at least to that of a ridotto in a second-rate Italian town, was as sure to excite notice and attract passengers, as a flaming candle every moth and father-longlegs in its neighbourhood. We were, therefore, in no want of company.

Our tea-table, which we had prudently established as far beyond the influence of Doctor Ehrhart's regale as possible, was soon surrounded by all the fashion not under immediate medical restraint that happened to be at the Caldas: old buckram officers, not much the wiser for having served under the Count de la Lippe; pot-bellied fidalgos, who had not yet been stewed down to less unseemly proportions; and desembargadors and men of the law, as greedy as sharks, and as heavy as cart-horses.

One of the most ponderous of the set, a personage of some political importance, and a distinguished graduate of the University of Coimbra, was half inclined to turn restive, because I would not sit down by him and explain in minute detail some passages in Blackstone's Commentaries about which he was eager of information. Pushing my chair away from this determined bore, he pushed his after me with such vehemence, that a conflict must have ensued, perhaps to my total discomfiture, had not his chair been killed under him; – both back and legs gave way, and down he fell flat on the gritty floor. Everybody's sides in the room shook with laughter – even the spare ribs of the Count de la Lippe's ancient martinet officers.

TENTH DAY

Knavish Provedore.—Leave the Caldas.—Obidos.—Aboriginal-looking hamlet.—Exquisite Atmosphere.—Pastoral Hymns to St. Anthony.—Bonfires on the Eve of his Festival.—Reception at Cadafaiz.—Delightful change.

June 12

We have been all cheated at a ferocious rate by one of those harpies called provedores, who, under the mask of administering justice, and superintending hospitals, and so forth, contrive to divert every little rill of royal beneficence into their own pockets. This knave was so accustomed to the sweets of monopolies, that he bought up half the fowls, turkeys, and provisions in the place, and then dealt them out to our numerous caravan at his own price. I refused seeing this cormorant; which was lucky, as I understood he joins insolence to knavery, – a compound which would have called forth my best manual exertions, occasioned delay, and very probably given but too much employment to Doctor Ehrhart.

It was so delightful a morning, – so temperate, for there were not any clouds – so balsamic, for a slight shower had lately fallen, – that I could not find it in my heart to be out of humour long. We had not left the Caldas in arrear half an hour, before we saw Obidos, with its towers and battlemented walls, rising above a forest of pines, and connected with the neighbouring hills by a long stretch of aqueduct. These hills being clothed with a thick vegetation of dwarf ilex, and myrtle, look at a distance as uniformly green as if covered with turf.

Cercal, where our dinner was prepared, is a pleasant little assemblage of reed-covered sloping sheds and pointed hovels, at the feet of shrubby acclivities. Before the entrance of this aboriginal-looking hamlet, is an irregular lawn, bounded by inclosures with bamboo fences, twined over with convolvuli of various colours, forming a labyrinth of cheerful lanes, through which whole families of turkeys, consequential fathers, bustling mothers, slim aunts, and half-fledged cousins, were wandering about, clucking, and whistling, and gobbling, with all the well-known volubility of their native language.

Though mid-day and in mid-June, the heat was moderate; the sky, of a pale tender blue, inexpressibly serene and beautiful. To breathe the soft air of such a climate, is in itself no trifling luxury; it seemed to inspire new life into every vein: and if to those gifts of Nature the blessings of a free government and the refinements of art were added, more philosophy than I am master of would be required, not to murmur at the shortness of our existence.

Our road in the evening lay between lofty slopes partially covered with bushes of rosemary and lavender in the fullest bloom. The sun went down behind the chain of hills which form the coast of the sea, just as we reached a quinta belonging to Forjaz, at present governor of Madeira. As we approached the rich cultivated plains framed in by the hills around Cadafaiz, we heard the country people, men, women, and children, singing hymns to Saint Anthony as they returned home from reaping.

Near Carregado we left the high road to take that of Cadafaiz. The whole country was blazing with fires in honour of tomorrow's festival. I counted above one hundred shining bright amongst the olive-trees; whilst a number of grotesque figures, withered hags, and meagre implings, kept glancing about before them, in the style of those visions the illuminati often contrive to conjure up, to delude and bamboozle their dupes and victims.

At Cadafaiz itself, that most comfortable of rustic manorial mansions, the Prior of St. Vincent's, who had preceded us above an hour in his light chaise, drawn by two potent mules, was waiting our arrival. The Prior of Aviz uttered a hearty 'thank God,' as he sunk down in an arm-chair of most ample dimensions. Dr. Ehrhart recommended us all to dilute, after his example, as freely as possible; and Franchi unpacked his pianoforte. Recollections of the Caldas and all its apothecaries, – not to mention its dust, its glare, its bustle, and its onions, – made me value the calm and cleanliness of this retired abode still more highly. O the delightful, refreshing change! Were I to live as many years as I have often been wished to do by my good friends the Spaniards, I should not forget how keenly I enjoyed it.

ELEVENTH DAY

Excursion to a Franciscan Convent.—A Miracle.—Country resembling Palestine.—Innumerable Assemblage of Peasants.—Their sincere Devotion.—Sublime Sight.—Observations of the Prior of Aviz.—The Benediction.—Ancient Portuguese Hymn.—Its grand effect on the present occasion.—Perilous Descent from the Mountain.—A Mandate from the Prince.—Evening.—Music and a Morisco Dance.

June 13

I shook off laziness manfully, not above an hour after sunrise; so did the Grand Prior of Aviz; – an effort, our hospitable host observed, worthy to be classed amongst the choicest of St. Anthony's miracles. Not a member of our caravan but seemed to feel the Saint's benign and holy influence. One would have thought it pervaded the very atmosphere; for even Dr. Ehrhart – no ardent devotee – desired to join our solemn pilgrimage to the Franciscan convent, on the summit of an exceedingly high hill, where the grand mass of the day was to be celebrated. The good Doctor having promised not to stop our procession by getting out of his vehicle and botanizing by the road-side, we set forth, after a slight breakfast, and wound our long array up the acclivity by a tedious, serpentine, rugged track.

We had attained a sort of resting-place, not more than one hundred yards beneath the summit, when a stout lubber, dressed in goats' skins, carrying a sickly brat in his arms, bolted forth from between two thorny bushes, looking like one possessed, and bawling out, 'A miracle! a miracle! My child was at the point of death, when the saint appeared to me in a dream, and told me to give it the raspings of a cow-horn: I did – and there you see it is alive and hearty.'

Hearty at least were Dr. Ehrhart's expressions of surprise at this most pastoral remedy; he kept repeating 'raspings of cow-horn, raspings of cow-horn!' so often, that I beseeched him, for St. Anthony's sake, to remain quiet; and we proceeded, the lout with his brat, having joined the great concourse of people on the top of the hill, still crying out, 'A miracle! a miracle!' and I am happy to add, for the honour of faith, my most perfect conviction that not a soul of the crowd – and a great crowd it was – but firmly believed him.

Arrived at length at the point to which we had been tending, I fancied myself suddenly transported to Palestine: a plain perfectly flat and arid presented itself, diversified alone by the low columned arcades and belfries of the convent, inclining to the ruinous, and bearing a strong resemblance in form and tint to the views I have seen of the semi-gothic chapels and cells at Jerusalem and Nazareth. Scattered all over from one end to the other of this extensive level, (for it stretched out above a mile,) were droves of asses, a few mules of superior caste glaringly caparisoned, and peasants without number, of all ages and sexes, sitting in clusters upon the ground, employed as busily in gathering together the fragments of a general repast, as if they had just partaken of some miraculous supply of loaves and fishes.

This was all mighty well, and admirably adapted to prompt a desire of sketching, for nothing could be more picturesque than these varied groups; but the comfort of comforts was to witness how gratefully devout they appeared, how perfectly convinced that they stood under the open eye of the Saint, and that by acting in conformity with his precepts, they might deserve, at the inevitable hour, his efficacious patronage. In the mean time I saw no tokens of riot or intemperance, no brandishing of knives, no drunken disputes or wallowings.

When the bells of the convent gave notice that service was going to begin, the groups that were scattered over the plain rapidly joined together, and moved in one dense body, one vast multitude, six or seven thousand at least, to the wide naked space before the entrance to the church, which, though not inconsiderable in its dimensions, was far too small to contain a twentieth part of so numerous a congregation.

The community, consisting of from thirty to forty monks, all young men, many with features as regular as the fine Grecian heads on the Syracusan medals, but looking pale and attenuated, were standing on the long line of steps. Their superior presented the banner of the Saint to my revered companions, who having saluted it with profound reverence, we entered the church. I looked back from the portal upon the multitude, which extended itself like a sea to a great distance; all silent, all kneeling, all with their moistened and glistening eyes (far many wept through religious fervour) fixed on the illumination which streamed from the high altar, and which appeared to them, I have no doubt, a cheering light, a sacred pharos, shining to conduct them to that haven where the ardent in faith and the contrite in spirit meet their eternal reward.

'Oh!' said the excellent Prior of Aviz to me, as he pressed my hand with parental kindness, 'this is a sight which relieves and elevates my heart. How glowing and sincere the piety of these plain countrymen! how consolatory their firm confidence in protection from above! And yet these warm, ennobling feelings – feelings which raise our nature above the dust – are precisely those the vile sycophants of the evil principle, the blood-stained monsters of France, pant to eradicate. The suppressors of institutions which tend to soothe those lacerating cares humanity is subject to, and to absorb in the glorious prospect of the future the corroding misery of the present, are, in fact, suppressors of happiness, – the delegates of that dread invisible agency, which, under an endless variety of specious masks, is ever in movement, seeking whom and what it may devour.'

Not one word had I to say against this reasoning; for how often have I thought myself, that these experiments upon the human mind, to which the Prior of Aviz alluded, are as abhorrent to men of pure and kindly feeling, as those of the hellish Majendie upon the unoffending animals he submits to the most horrible and lingering torture, and for purposes equally problematical.

The 'Ite, missa est' having been pronounced, the Prior of Aviz, trembling with emotion and evidently much affected, was conducted in procession by the monks to their sacristy, to put on his pontifical vestments, and, next, to the steps before the entrance, where, looking up to the effigy on the banner, again displayed by the superior of the convent, he bestowed, as if immediately delegated by the Saint himself to perform that sacred office, a solemn, heartfelt benediction.

At that moment, when every knee was bent and every head was bowed, the ancient and venerable hymn appointed for this festival, so dear to the natives of Portugal – so often sung by their armies in their proud days of conquest on the eve of going into battle, rose with one accord, as from one heart, from the whole of the vast assemblage. The perfect unison of so many thousand manly voices, mingled with the clearer tones of children and their mothers, filled the summer air with a volume of sound more intellectually harmonious than any which ever reached my ear from the artificial efforts of musicians and choristers. Prayer does not always ascend with the greatest fervency from beneath gilded vaults or gorgeous cupolas; it is in the free untainted desert, under Nature's own sky, that man seems to commune more deeply with his God. Impressed with that sentiment, the bare rocks, the scattered stones, the withered turf, ranked higher in my estimation than all the splendours of regal magnificence; and the simple congregation assembled together in this wild and desolate place to thank the Almighty for his blessings, appeared far superior in my eyes to those pharisaic gatherings attracted to church by worldly motives and the parade of idle vanity.

So very thick was the concourse of people, and so profoundly were they affected by the late most solemn benediction, that it was no easy matter for the prelate to pass between their still kneeling groups to regain the sacristy in order to be divested of his heavy cope, the people pressing forwards to kiss his hand in such tides, and with such earnestness, that he felt fatigued and jaded. Nor was his lassitude, destined to a speedy termination: he had hardly resumed his customary habiliments, when our egress from the church was absolutely impeded by a procession of young lads, dressed in a style as antique as the Moorish domination in Portugal; some carrying baskets of fruit and corn; some, on an ornamented sledge, an immense mass of wax fashioned into the shape of a gigantic taper; and some, a number of lambs bedecked with ribands and flowers.

I thought, when I saw presented on the steps before the altar these living offerings, not one of which I understood, to my heart's content, was devoted to the knife, but all destined to be reared with care and tenderness – I thought even their bleatings might reach the throne of universal beneficence. We well know how positively the inspired David declares, in one of his Psalms, that the ear of God is open to the supplications of all his creatures, to whom, as well as to us, he has imparted the blessings of light, of sleep, and of nutriment, – 'qui dat jumentis escam ipsorum et pullis corvorum invocantibus eum.'

When I communicated to my revered friend the feelings which throbbed in my own bosom, and reminded him of the fervid effusion of the prophet king, he replied: 'Most entirely do I sympathise with the holy monarch. Man, in the delusion of pride, may arrogate to himself an exclusive supremacy; but fully persuaded am I, that the same principle of life which animates the wisest and brightest of mankind, pervades the boundless creation in all its forms and branches; and when that principle prompts the cry of distress or the expression of gratitude in the humblest animal, neither pass unheeded by the Divine Creator, nor are they poured forth to him in vain. These are my own interior sentiments,' continued the venerable prelate. 'And they are mine also,' I could not repress exclaiming.

At length the procession, after depositing all its offerings, having retired into the secret courts and penetralia of the convent, the crowd began to disperse; a passage was cleared between the remaining groups of the multitude, and we regained our carriages, much to the relief of the Grand Prior, who was experiencing an almost total exhaustion.

What with the sun-rays from above, and the rolling stones below, our descent was not only broiling, but dangerous: many of our mules stumbled, and one fell down dead, half crushing the driver in its fall. The stoppage and confusion this sad accident occasioned in one of the narrowest parts of our perilous track exposed us to scorching heat for half an hour. We arrived at last at our cool, shady quarters, as brown as mummies, and as dry as cinders.

The first living objects that met us at the massive portal, surmounted by a huge marble cross, which defends the entrance of the orange orchard immediately around the mansion, were two special couriers in the royal livery, magnificently badged and booted, just arrived with a written mandate from the Prince, summoning the two Priors to an audience tomorrow at the palace of Queluz, precisely at three. They delivered me also a very kind letter of invitation from the Marquis of Anjeja (then lord in waiting) to dine with him at the same hour.

'Really,' said our most amiable host, a little ruffled by this peremptory command, 'we did not expect a summons to communicate observations upon Alcobaça so soon, – on our way home, too, God bless us! without being allowed time to shake off the dust from our garments, and make ourselves decent and comfortable. But an uncontrollable love of gossip is inherent in the character of royalty, and as indelible: we have nothing to do but to obey.'

So saying, and so sighing, with many an ejaculation from the inmost soul of laziness, both Priors wrote answers to the royal mandate; I did the same to the Marquis of Anjeja, and the couriers departed.

After every comfort and ablution our pleasant retired chambers could afford, we partook of a delicious repast, and of all the blandishments which delicate dishes and iced sherbets could bestow on the willing palate. To these delights succeeded, on the part of the Lord Priors at least, a most comfortable nap, and then a stroll in the long-bowered alleys of the quinta; and then the evening perfume of orange-flowers and jasmine, and the evening song of birds, – music, also, from Franchi, accompanied on the guitar by two novices, who played from their heart and soul most ravishingly, – and then a dance of true oriental fervour, performed by a chosen band of the morisco-dressed processionists, who had been drawn down, not from heaven, like the Angel to St. Cecilia, but from the convent on the hill; where, I have little doubt, their freaks and gambols were sadly missed, and the temporary deprivation of such amusing frolics heartily regretted.

TWELFTH DAY

Dreary expanse of Country between Cadafaiz and Queluz.—Arrival at the Palace.—Court Lumber.—Observations of the Marquis of Anjeja relative to the Prince-Regent.—Promised Audience of his Royal Highness.—Visit to the Forbidden Gardens.—Surprise of an African Gardener.—A Pavilion.—Nightscene.—Preparations for a Fete.—The Infanta's Nymph-like Attendants.—The young Marquis of Marialva.—Interview with her Royal Highness.—A Race.—A Dance.—The Prince's Summons.—Conversation with him.—Character of that Sovereign.—Baneful influence of his despotic Consort.—Unhappy Aspirants to Court Benefits.—Private Conference with the Marquis.—The Prince-Regent's Afflictions.—His Vision.—

Anjeja's urgent Request.—Terrible Cries from the Queen—Their effect on me.—My Departure from the Palace.

14th June

The morning was the very essence of summer – and summer in Portugal, consequently tremendously hot. Such heat was oppressive enough, but the Grand Prior thought early rising still more abominable, and notwithstanding the Prior of St. Vincent's exhortations to set forth whilst any degree of coolness lingered in the atmosphere, there was no persuading him to move before half-past eight.

Being myself pretty well seasoned to meridian excursions, and bronzed all over like a native Portuguese, I set the sun at defiance, mounted my Arabian, and steering my course as directly as was possible without the aid of a compass, traversed the wide expanse of country between Cadafaiz and Queluz; – and a sad dreary expanse it was, exhibiting only now and then a straggling flock, looking pretty and pastoral – a neglected quinta of orange-trees with its decaying garden-house, the abode of crime or innocence, whichever you like best to fancy – or a half-ruined windmill, with its tattered vans, revolving lackadaisically in the languid and feeble breeze.

Exactly at the hour named, I arrived, not a little ennuied and wearied, at the palace of Queluz. The chaises belonging to the Priors of Aviz and St. Vincent's were waiting before the royal entrance, for both prelates were still closeted with the Prince Regent. Blessing Heaven that I had nothing to do with the business, whatever it might be, that was in agitation, I gladly took refuge from the intolerable sunshine in the apartments allotted to the lord in waiting; – shabby enough they were, bare as many an English country church, and not much less dingy.

The beings who were wandering about this limbo, or intermediate state, belonged chiefly to that species of living furniture which encumber royal palaces – walking chairs, animated screens, commodes and conveniences, to be used by sovereigns in any manner they like best; men who had little to feed on besides hope, and whose rueful physiognomies showed plainly enough the wasting effects of that empty diet, – weather-beaten equerries, superannuated véadors, and wizened pages. The whole party were yawning over dusty card-tables.

Making them many low bows, which were returned with equal courtesy, I passed forward into an interior apartment, where the Marquis of Anjeja and his son the Conde de Villaverde were waiting for me, and immediately dinner was served up. Our repast was not particularly distinguished by good cheer or lively conversation.

As soon as it was over, and the motley tribe of attendants who had crowded tumultuously round – our table sent about their no business at all, the Marquis observed to me in a very subdued and rather melancholy tone, that the Prince had been greatly disturbed of late by strange apprehensions and stranger dreams; that his temper was much ruffled, and that something, he could not tell what, bore heavily on his mind. He would have entered, I believe, into further details of still greater importance, had not a page called him away to the royal presence.

'I shall return in half an hour,' said he, 'and finish what I had to say to you.' This half hour exceeded three quarters, and two quarters added to that; but they passed rapidly, for both the young Conde and myself, oppressed by a warm atmosphere, and lulled by the drone of bumble-bees, and the monotonous buzzing of courtiers and lacqueys, in the adjoining apartments, had fallen fast asleep.

When I awoke from this happy state of forgetfulness, one of my servants, who had followed me from Cadafaiz with a change of dress, took me into a room which a principal attendant of the palace had given up to him, and out of which I issued completely renovated, and met the Marquis hastily bearing to me the interesting intelligence, that in the course of the evening, or as soon after nightfall as possible, the Prince Regent would give me an audience. 'In the intervening time,' he added, 'if you wish to see the curious birds and flowers last sent from the Brazils, the gardens, though accessible of late to very few persons, shall be open to you. Villaverde would most gladly accompany you, but even he has not been in the habit of straying about them for some time past. As to myself, the Prince has a long series of deputations and petitions to receive, and it is my duty to remain near his royal person on these occasions so pardon my not offering myself as your guide. At the extremity of the avenue you see from these windows, stands a pavilion well worthy your attention, and I rather wish you might principally employ it in examining the paintings and china, till the moment arrives when the Prince will be at leisure to receive you.'

I bowed, the Marquis and his son bowed also, and I entered the grand avenue, wondering what in the name of mystery all these precautions could mean. The enigma was not long in meeting with some explanation. A gardener, who had left my service only last year, and was now established prime guardian of carnations and anemones in this regal paradise, advanced towards me with looks of the greatest surprise, and touching the extremities of my garments with his exuberant lips – for he was neither more nor less than a negro – stammered out, 'Most excellent sir, by what chance do I see you here, where so few are permitted to enter?' 'By the chance of having the Prince's permission.'

'Ah, sir,' continued he, 'it is the Princess who reigns here almost exclusively.'

'Well,' answered I, 'her indignation, I hope, will not visit me too severely: here I am, and here I shall continue.'

With a low salam in the style of a regular Bostangi, the poor African, not a little confounded, humbly retired, and left me at full liberty to enter the pavilion, whose richly gilded trellised doors stood wide open. Many entertaining objects, arabesque paintings by Costa full of fire and fancy, and mandarin josses of the most supreme and ridiculous ugliness, kept me so well amused that half an hour glided away pretty smoothly.

The evening was now drawing towards its final close, and the groves, pavilions, and aviaries sinking apace into shadow: a few wandering lights sparkled amongst the more distant thickets, – fire-flies perhaps – perhaps meteors; but they did not disturb the reveries in which I was wholly absorbed.

'So then,' thought I within myself, 'the Infanta Donna Carlotta is become the predominant power in these lovely gardens, once so profusely adorned and fondly cherished by the late kind-hearted and saintly king. She is now Princess of Brazil and Princess Regent; and what besides, Heaven preserve me from repeating!'

Reports, I well knew, not greatly to the good fame of this

exalted personage, had been flying about, numerous as butterflies; some dark-coloured, like the wings of the death-head moth, and some brilliant and gay, like those of the fritillaria.

This night I began to perceive, from a bustle of preparation already visible in the distance, that a mysterious kind of fete was going forwards; and whatever may have been the leading cause, the effect promised at least to be highly pleasing. Cascades and fountains were in full play; a thousand sportive *jets d'eau* were sprinkling the rich masses of bay and citron, and drawing forth all their odours, as well-taught water is certain to do upon all such occasions. Amongst the thickets, some of which received a tender light from tapers placed low on the ground under frosted glasses, the Infanta's nymph-like attendants, all thinly clad after the example of her royal and nimble self, were glancing to and fro, visible one instant, invisible the next, laughing and talking all the while with very musical silver-toned voices. I fancied now and then I heard gruffer sounds, but perhaps I was mistaken. Be that as it pleases Lucifer, just as I was advancing to explore a dusky labyrinth, out came, all of a sudden, my very dear friend Don Pedro, the young Marquis of Marialva.

'What! at length returned from Alcobaça,' said he, lifting me a foot off the ground in a transport of jubilation; 'where is my uncle?'

'Safe enough,' answered I, perhaps indiscreetly: 'he had his audience five or six hours ago, and is gone home snug to his cushions and *calda da galinha*. I am waiting for my turn.'

Which will not come so soon as you imagine,' replied Don Pedro, 'for the Prince is retired to his mother's apartments, and how long he may be detained there no one can tell. But in the mean while come with me. The Princess, who has learnt you are here, and who has heard that you run like a greyhound, wishes to be convinced herself of the truth of a report she thinks so extraordinary.'

'Nothing so easy,' said I, taking him by the hand; and we sprang forwards, not to the course immediately, but to an amphitheatre of verdure concealed in the deepest recess of the odoriferous thickets, where, seated in the oriental fashion on a rich velvet carpet spread on the grass, I beheld the Alcina of the place, surrounded by thirty or forty young women, every one far superior in loveliness of feature and fascination of smile to their august mistress.

'How did you leave the fat waddling monks of Alcobaça,' said her royal highness. 'I hope you did not run races with them; – but that would indeed have been impossible. There,' continued she, 'down that avenue, if you like, when I clap my hands together, start; your friend Pedro and two of my donzellas shall run with you – take care you are not beaten.'

The avenue allotted for this amusing contest was formed of catalpas and orange trees, and as completely smooth and level as any courser, biped or quadruped, upon whom all the bets in the universe were depending, could possibly desire. The signal given, my youthful friend, all ardour, all agility, and two Indian-looking girls of fourteen or fifteen, the very originals, one would have thought, of those graceful creatures we often see represented in Hindoo paintings, darted forth with amazing swiftness. Although I had given them ten paces in advance, exerting myself in right earnest, I soon left them behind, and reached the goal – a marble statue, rendered faintly visible by lamps gleaming through transparent vases. I thought I heard a murmur of approbation; but it was so kept down, under the terror of disturbing the queen, as to be hardly distinguishable.

'Muy bien, muy bien,' said the Princess in her native Castilian, when we returned to the margin of the velvet carpet upon which she was still sitting reclined, and made our profound obeisances. 'I see the Englishman can run – report has not deceived me. Now,' continued her royal highness, 'let me see whether he can dance a bolero; they say he can, and like one of us if that be true – and I hope it is, for I abhor unsuccessful enterprises – Antonita shall be his partner, – and she is by far the best dancer that followed me from Spain.'

This command had been no sooner issued, than a low, soft-flowing choir of female voices, without the smallest dissonance, without the slightest break, – smooth, well-tuned, and perfectly melodious, – filled my ear with such enchantment, that I glided along in a delirium of romantic delight.

My partner, an Andalusian, as full of fire and animation as the brightest beauties of Cadiz and Seville, though not quite so young as I could have wished her to be, was rattling her castanets at a most intrepid rate, and raising her voice to a higher pitch than was seemly in these regions, when a universal 'Hush, hush, hush!' arrested our movements, suspended the harmonious notes of the choir, and announced the arrival of the Marquis of Anjeja. After a thousand kind and courteous compliments he was pleased to pay me, he begged another thousand pardons of the Princess for having ventured to interrupt her recreations: 'But, madam,' continued he, 'the Prince Regent has been waiting several minutes for the Englishman, and I leave you to judge whether he has a minute to lose.'

Her Royal Highness looked rather blank at this intelligence, and, compassionating my disappointment, held out her hand, which I kissed with fervour, and three or four of her attendants as many silken handkerchiefs, which I found very convenient in removing those dews which not only the night, but such violent exercise as I had lately taken, occasioned. Panting, and almost breathless, I quitted the enchanted circle with great reluctance.

What a contrast the dark, dull ante-chambers of the palace presented to that lively and graceful scene! It was in the long state gallery where the Prince habitually receives the homage of the court upon birthdays and festivals, – a pompous, richly gilded apartment, set round with colossal vases of porcelain, as tall and as formal as grenadiers, – that his Royal Highness was graciously pleased to grant me audience.

He was standing alone in this vast room, thoughtful, it appeared to me, and abstracted. He seemed, however, to brighten upon my approach; and although he was certainly the reverse of handsome, there was an expression of shrewdness, and at the same time benignity, in his very uncommon countenance, singularly pleasing: it struck me that he had a decided look, particularly about the mouth, of his father's maternal ancestors. John the Fifth having married the Archduchess, daughter of the Emperor Charles the Sixth, he had therefore an hereditary claim to those wide-spreading, domineering lips, which so remarkably characterised the House of Austria, before it merged into that of Lorraine.

'Welcome back from Alcobaça!' said his Royal Highness to me, with the most condescending kindness: 'I hope your journey was pleasant – how did you find the roads?'

'Not half so bad as I expected, especially upon our return from the great convent, the reverend fathers having summoned all their numerous dependents to mend them with astonishing expedition: the Lord Abbot took care of that.'

'He takes excellent care of himself, at least,' observed the Prince, – 'nobody better. Is it not true that he is become most gloriously corpulent, and fallen passionately in love with the fine French cookery you gave him an opportunity of enjoying?'

I perceived by this sally that the Grand Prior had been a faithful narrator of our late proceedings, as was proved more and more by the following queries.

'You had a stage-play too, had you not? The fathers at Mafra have often regaled me with performances of a similar nature; and many a hearty laugh have I had at them, and with them, before now. I dare say you must have thought them half out of their senses; their poet particularly, who, I hear, is one of the most ridiculous buffoons, the most impudent blockhead *(tolerað)* in the kingdom. I shall send for him one of these days myself; they say he is highly diverting, and I want something to cheer my spirits. Every despatch from France brings us such frightful intelligence, that I am lost in amazement and horror; the ship of the state in every country in Europe is labouring under a heavy torment, – God alone can tell upon what shore we shall be all drifted!'

With these prophetic words, most solemnly and energetially pronounced, the Prince thought, fit to dismiss me, honouring me again with those affable expressions of regard which his excellent heart never failed to dictate. Let me observe, whilst the recollections of the interviews I have had with this beneficent sovereign remain fresh in my memory, that not one of his subjects spoke their native language – that beautiful harmonious language, with greater purity and eloquence than himself. When in his graver moods, there was a promptitude, a facility in his diction, most remarkable every word he uttered was to the purpose, and came with the fullest force. When he chose to relax, – which he certainly was apt enough to do more than now and then, – a quaint national turn of humour added a zest to his pleasantries, that, upon my entering heart and soul into the idiom of the language, has often afforded me capital entertainment. No one knew how to win popular affection, after its own fashion, more happily than this well-intentioned, single-minded prince. Had it not been for the baneful influence of his despotic consort, – her restless intrigues of all hues, political as well as private – her wanton freaks of favouritism and atrocious acts of cruelty, – his reign would have gone down to the latest times in the annals of his kingdoms surrounded with a halo of gratitude.

Upon my reaching the great portal of this silent gallery, and fumbling to open its valves – for this extremity of the apartment was but very feebly illuminated, – the Marquis, who had been giving some orders to somebody of whom I only caught a glimpse, spared me the trouble of further rattlings at locks or door-knobs, and we entered together another shadowy world – another immense saloon. Here, by the wan light of one solitary lustre, containing but half its complement of yellowish wax tapers drooping with dismal snuffs, I discovered some fifteen or twenty unhappy aspirants to court benefits still loitering and lingering about. The sovereign of Portugal was at this period as completely despotic as the most decided amateur of unlimited monarchy could possibly desire: they who entered these palace regions came with as many hopes of success and fears of the contrary as if they were resorting to a table of hazard. The sovereign, in their eyes, was Chance personified; his decrees for or against you, modestly styled *avisos,* were pieces of advice to the judicial obeyers of his commands, which, if once obtained, were never slighted.

Most of the victims of this system, at this time in this great hall assembled, appeared visibly suffering under the sickness of hope deferred. 'Five hours have I been walking up and down, to and fro, to no purpose,' said an old General, my very particular acquaintance. 'Is there no chance yet of delivering my memorial into his royal highness's own hand?' whispered another veteran, decorated with scars as well as orders; 'None,' answered the Marquis: 'the Prince is retired for the night, and you had better follow his example.'

Had there been more light, we should have been fastened upon by a greater number of petitioners; but, thanks to the pervading gloom, we slipped along half-undiscovered.

Our next movements were directed through an ante-chamber of large size and much simplicity, for its walls were quite plain, and the roof as unornamented as that of a barn. A few expiring lamps gave me an opportunity of perceiving another assemblage of the votaries of royal favour in some of its shapes, less dignified than the company we had just quitted, but who had been equally eager, and who now were equally exhausted, – country magistrates, sea captains, provincial noblesse, and I know not who besides; some of them, if truth may be spoken, looking more like the *bad* than the *beau* idéal of bandits and bravoes; but what they were in reality, thank God, I am perfectly ignorant. Anjeja paid them no attention as we passed on through their opening ranks: his looks, though not his voice, told me plainly enough,

Non ragionam di lor,
Ma guarda e passa.

These looks seemed to tell me at the same time that he wished to converse with me in private.

I was tired of close conferences in close apartments; I longed for the refreshing sea-breezes of my quinta on the banks of the Tagus; the very name of which (San José de Ribamar) was music to my ears at this moment. A page announced that my carriages, just arrived from Cadafaiz, were in waiting. This was tantalizing indeed: I would have taken leave of my most obliging Marquis without any very deep regret after all, but he would not let me off so soon as I eagerly desired; he absolutely insisted upon taking me into an interior apartment I had never visited before, where we sat down, – for here, at least, were plenty of chairs and sofas, and he addressed me with considerable emotion in the following manner:

'You see, his royal highness is more gloomy than he used to be.'

'Upon the whole,' answered I, 'his spirits are less depressed than I was led to imagine: my friends the Priors seem to have regaled him with many a good story about convents, for he laughed several times at my Lord Almoner's charities of all kinds beginning so comfortably at home.'

'Ah!' replied Anjeja, 'you little think, notwithstanding this apparent levity, what an accumulated weight of sorrows press him down: he is the most affectionate of sons, the most devoted; and being such, feels for his mother's sufferings with the acutest poignancy. Those sufferings are frightfully severe, more heart-rending than any words of mine can express. This very evening he knelt by the Queen's couch above two hours, whilst, in a paroxysm of mental agony, she kept crying out for mercy, imagining that, in the midst of a raging flame which enveloped the whole chamber, she beheld her father's image a calcined mass of cinder, – a statue in form like that in the Terreiro do Paco, but in colour black and horrible, – erected on a pedestal of molten iron, which a crowd of ghastly phantoms – she named them, I shall not – were in the act of dragging down. This vision haunts her by night and by day; and should she continue to describe it in all its horrible details again and again to my royal master, I fear his brain will catch fire too. There is a remedy – my relation, her confessor, knows it well – there is a medicine, and of the highest and most salutary kind – such might be administered – restitutions might be made – infernal acts revoked, and justice rendered. But hitherto the powers of evil – certain demons in the shape of some of Pombal's ancient counsellors, and others equally culpable, though not so old in iniquity, have impeded measures which would conciliate the disaffected, and although they might excite the gibes and murmurs of the disciples of new doctrines would attach all us, the ancient nobles of the realm, to the House of Braganza more closely than ever. May I ask, has the Prince ever touched upon this subject to you? I think Marialva told me he had, and once in his presence.'

I answered, 'If he did, it was ambiguously, and with so much slightness that it passed like a fleeting cloud.'

After a long pause, during which Anjeja appeared lost in thought, he said to me with the greatest earnestness, 'If, at the next audience the Prince may give you, he should pour forth his sorrows for his mother's malady into your bosom, – which I have reason to conjecture he shortly may, for I know that he feels himself towards you affectionately well inclined' (*sumamente affeiçoado*), 'remember the kind regard you entertain for our family,' (he meant the Noronhas in general, from which great house all the Marialvas are paternally descended) 'remember to let it suggest such observations as may further a great and interesting cause. I wish also you would dwell particularly on what the late Archbishop, your devoted friend, may probably have said to you upon this subject. Whatever that may have been, give it the turn we wish, and do not let it lose any charm in the narration.'

I could hardly repress a smile at this urgent request to launch forth beyond the exact limits of truth, if not of probability; for I perfectly recollected the good Archbishop's opinions were everything but favourable to the reversal of those attainders. However, I preserved a decorous gravity. I said nothing; but I contrived that my looks should express a disposition to second his wishes the first opportunity of doing so that might present itself.

At this moment, the most terrible, the most agonizing shrieks – shrieks such as I hardly conceived possible – shrieks more piercing than those which rung through the Castle of Berkeley, when Edward the Second was put to the most cruel and torturing death – inflicted upon, me a sensation of horror such as I never felt before. The Queen herself, whose apartment was only two rooms off from the chamber in which we were sitting, uttered those dreadful sounds: 'Ai Jesous! Ai Jesous!' did she exclaim again and again in the bitterness of agony.

I believe I turned pale; for Anjeja said to me, 'I see how deeply you are affected: think what the sufferings must be that prompt such cries; think what a son must feel, and such a son as our royal master.'

I undoubtedly thought all this, and a great deal more: not only the tears in my eyes, but the faltering of my voice, expressed the intensity of my feelings. The Marquis, far from displeased at the effect produced upon me, embraced me with redoubled kindness. Notwithstanding my entreaties for him to remain in his apartment, he was determined, after I had taken leave, to conduct me to the outward door of the palace; nor did he cease gazing, I was afterwards told, upon the carriage which bore me away, till the sound of the wheels grew fainter and fainter, and even the torches which were borne before it became invisible.

NOTES

I.
—Theatre in a distant part of the Convent, p.41.

My readers need not start at the idea of a play in a convent, and a synod of reverend fathers assisting at its representation. Such entertainments were often resorted to at Mafra to dispel the profound ennui of that royal and monastic residence – the Escurial of Portugal. Upon these occasions, the actors, orchestra, and audience were all monks, with the exception of his late Majesty, John the Sixth, and a few especial lay favourites.

II.
—Grotto-like communications, p.56.

The lively and intelligent Miss Pardoe's charming description of her visit to this famous convent, subsequent to the predatory incursion of the French, and previous to its final desecration by their imitators, the modern Portuguese, cannot be too warmly commended. She paints the supreme beauty of the young monk she caught a peep at (p.77), and who manifested himself more fully, (see p. 89) in a fervid and animated style, which does credit to the discriminating eye of the fair and susceptible authoress. Her hints (p.100) of a subterranean road from the monastery of Alcobaça to a Bernardine nunnery in the neighbourhood, are far more palpable than any I can pretend to have received. They afford the finest play to the imagination. We immediately assign the handsome monk as beautiful a partner; and the picture becomes complete.

III.
—The Bird-Queen's garden, &c. pp.58–63.

This fine, trim garden was suffered to fall into total ruin, and its feathered inhabitants were dispersed and destroyed, upon the death of their mistress, which occurred about ten months after the period of my visit. The French armies, in their devastating marches and counter-marches through Portugal, completed the work of desolation, by cutting down the pine-forest, and grubbing up even the very roots for fuel.

IV.
—*The Monks of the Royal Monastery*, p.63.

The revenue of this royal monastery, at the period of my excursion to it, considerably exceeded 24,000*l* and the charities such wealth enabled the monks to dispense were most ample, and judiciously applied. The traces of John the Fifth's munificence were then visible in all their freshness and lustre. Since those golden days of reciprocal good-will and confidence between the landlord and the tenant, the master and the servant, what cruel and arbitrary inroads have been made upon individual happiness! What almost obsolete oppressions have been revived under new-fangled, specious names! What a cold and withering change, in short, has been perpetrated by a well-organized system of spoliation, tricked out in the plausible garb of philosophic improvement and general utility!

V.
—*Alfagiraõ*, p.65.

Tradition informs us that it was at this castle, which, from a distance at least, looks magnificently picturesque, that the good king Don Deniz sometimes held his splendid and opulent court. He was husband to St. Isabel, one of the purest gems of the Roman calendar. From this virtuous and exemplary queen descended the less saintly Constance of Castile, duchess of York. The accounts given by chroniclers of the wealth and prosperity of Don Deniz, the successful impulse he gave to agriculture, and the quantity of gold extracted under his auspices from the sands of the Tagus, appear incredible in our days of almost universal scepticism.

VI.
—*The hellish Majendie*, p.72.

I had copied, for insertion here, a record of these atrocious experiments, which appeared in most of the newspapers of the time, and were even alluded to in parliament; but, upon reading it over, although it would fully justify the epithet I have bestowed on this keen anatomist, the details are so heart-sickening, so horrible, that I shrink from their further dissemination.

VII.
—The young Marquis of Marialva, p.79.

From this mild night, I have been told repeatedly, may be traced the marked predilection of the future empress-queen for this graceful young nobleman – a predilection about which much has been said and more conjectured.